Praise for
GRANDILOQUENT WORDS

"This tome will be going straight into the front of my reference bookshelf. No self-respecting rapper or chap of letters should be suffonsified without it."

—MR. B, THE GENTLEMAN RHYMER

"A wonderfully curated reference for logophiles everywhere. It's a remarkable thing to make the mundane interesting. It's even more remarkable to do it one word at a time. Get yourself a sturdy shoehorn because you'll be dying to use every last one of these wonderful words."

—JONATHAN EDWARD DURHAM, author of *Winterset Hollow*

"*Yawmagorp?* That word sounds made up! News flash: *All* words are made up. Some just have more character than others. Jason Travis Ott has done a great service in expanding our vocabularies with *Grandiloquent Words*. Don't be a *yawmagorp*—'a lounging idler who yawns, gapes, and stretches'—and buy this book."

—JAMES FELL, author of *On This Day in History Sh!t Went Down*

"A thoroughly entertaining, charming, and informative book for anyone in love with the English language and its colorful history. The illustrations are also delightful throughout."

—PETER E. MELTZER, author of *The Thinker's Thesaurus*

"Jason Travis Ott delights us with the stories behind many lost gems of the English language. From *snerdle* to *pandiculate*, he offers a delicious feast of dolorifuges."

—KAREN PIERCE, author of *Recipes for Murder*

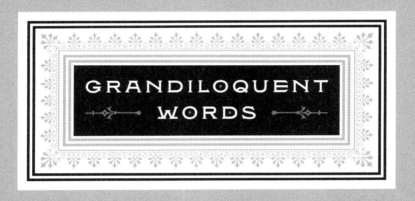

GRANDILOQUENT WORDS

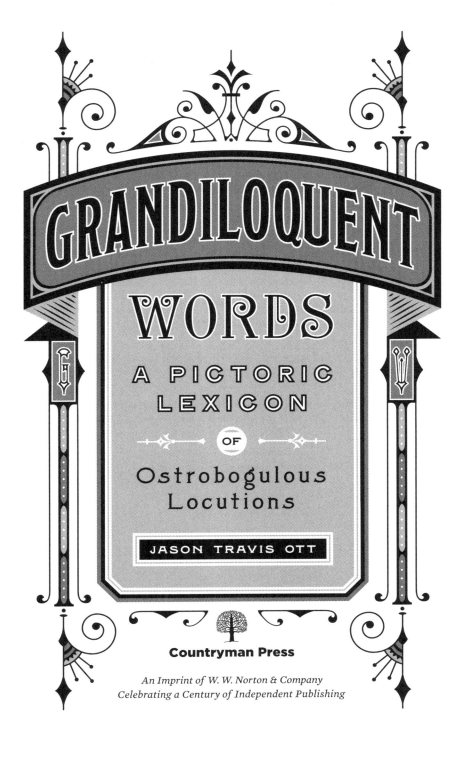

GRANDILOQUENT

WORDS

A PICTORIC LEXICON

OF

Ostrobogulous Locutions

JASON TRAVIS OTT

Countryman Press

An Imprint of W. W. Norton & Company
Celebrating a Century of Independent Publishing

Illustration credits: page 13: Harris Brisbane Dick Fund, 1937; page 35: Harris Brisbane Dick Fund, 1928; page 36: Harris Brisbane Dick Fund, 1928; page 106: National Portrait Gallery, Smithsonian Institution; page 108: Gift of Mrs. Yvonne Möen Cumerford, 1965; page 211: Rogers Fund, 1922; page 217: The Elisha Whittelsey Collection, The Elisha Whittelsey Fund, 1959

For information about permission to reproduce selections from this book, write to Permissions, Countryman Press, 500 Fifth Avenue, New York, NY 10110

For information about special discounts for bulk purchases, please contact W. W. Norton Special Sales at specialsales@wwnorton.com or 800-233-4830

Manufacturing by Versa Press
Book design by Raphael Geroni
Production manager: Devon Zahn

Countryman Press
www.countrymanpress.com

An imprint of W. W. Norton & Company, Inc.
500 Fifth Avenue, New York, NY 10110
www.wwnorton.com

978-1-68268-799-4

10 9 8 7 6 5 4 3 2 1

THIS BOOK IS DEDICATED TO MY WIFE AND MY
WHOLE LIFE, ANGIE. THERE WILL NEVER BE ENOUGH
WORDS TO TELL YOU HOW MUCH I LOVE YOU.

CONSTITUENTS
(Contents)

PREAMBLE
(Introduction)

"Nothing pleases an ignorant person more than a high-sounding term 'full of fury.' How melodious and drum-like are those vulgar coruscations *rumbumptious, slantingdicular, splendiferous, rumbustious,* and *ferricadouzer.* What a 'pull' the sharp-nosed lodging-house keeper thinks she has over her victims if she can but hurl such testimonies of a liberal education at them when they are disputing her charges, and threatening to *absquatulate!*"

—JOHN CAMDEN HOTTEN, *A Dictionary of Modern Slang, Cant, and Vulgar Words,* 1859

HERE IS GREAT POWER IN THE KNOWING OF A word. The controversial hypothesis of linguistic relativity holds that language shapes our perception of reality. That old saw about the Inuit language having 50 distinct words to describe snow—true, it turns out, depending on dialect—nicely illustrates this idea.

Language, verbal and nonverbal, has served us humans well in our evolution as a species. Our nature impels us to identify and classify what surrounds us. Our ancestors learned a long time ago that it's not a good idea to whack a hornet's nest with a stick. Language made it possible to share that helpful tidbit forward through time without every one of us having to find out the hard way for ourselves. Each generation receives language, uses and changes it, and teaches it to the next generation, which builds on it anew. Don't spit into the wind, don't climb into the gorilla enclosure at the zoo, wash your hands, don't go down dark alleyways alone, fasten your seat belt, wear the recommended personal protective equipment for the job at hand, et cetera, ad nauseum, ad infinitum.

The clans and tribes of the ancient world multiplied, migrated, and ultimately lost touch with one another. Isolation gave rise to linguistic divergence, and dialects evolved into distinct languages. Travelers couldn't understand the locals, which led to some interesting dining experiences (among other activities). Eventually, the drive for conquest and profit gave rise to the two "-aders": traders and invaders. Trade routes connected remote regions over vast distances, allowing for the dissemination and intermingling of ideas, philosophies, and of course words. Along the way, one linguistic group realized that another had words that their own language lacked, or they liked some of the other group's words better. Traditionalists in the adoptive group held tight to their stodgy, aging lexicons. Versions of "Those silly kids and their wacky new words!" have reverberated countless times through the forums of history. Those silly kids creatively combined those new words into fancier and harder-to-pronounce terms, giving rise to grandiloquent language that employs generations of dictionary writers, consternates spelling bee contestants, and holds my imagination in thrall.

I'm not a professional lexicographer; I don't even have a degree in English. But I collect words like someone's silly aunt who scours garage sales, thrift stores, and flea markets for Hummel figurines despite already owning at least three of each one ever made. Each fancy new word represents a tantalizing morsel of Turkish delight sans the White Witch. Picking up antiquated tomes—with their heady aroma of old paper and binder's glue perfuming the air—and finding fascinating new words thrill me.

My mother was a bibliophagist, and *The American Heritage Dictionary of the English Language* held pride of place on one of the bookshelves in our farmhouse. The sheer size of the tome and the index notches cut into the side for each letter drew my incipient curiosity. My solitary youth passed mostly ensconced in the stacks of the Mason City Public Library or meandering the exhibits of the Charles H. MacNider Art Museum, which also had a cozy little reading room. Around age 12, I gathered the courage to venture into the reference section, a mysterious inner sanctum filled with books so precious that nobody could remove them from the premises. One of my high school teachers, Terry Crane, a kind and generous soul, added fuel to the fire of my linguistic intrigue. A writer, he offhandedly quoted Shakespeare at the most apropos moments and delighted in confounding us students by phrasing common statements in grandiloquent ways. One such phrase that lingers in my memory pertained to the fruitless pursuit of a nondomesticated waterfowl of the family Anatidae whenever referring to a wild goose chase.

A couple of decades later, in 2012, I was perusing Facebook one fine day, looking for a quirky yet educational vocabulary page with which to amuse myself. Unable to find one that I liked, I posted a random word and its definition on my own timeline. Not even the virtual crickets chirruped; the post received not a single like. So I tried again the following day. The reverberating *womp, womp* of an imaginary sad trombone echoed in a void of apathy.

Prior to this disappointing foray, I'd created a page on which I posted some of my artwork, so I married the words to antique illustrations and started posting them there. Within a week, 15 new users started following me, but I wanted to keep my art separate from the words I was sharing. Thus was born Grandiloquent Word of the Day, an educational, entertaining, and illustrated online lexicon. From those humble beginnings, the page has grown into a community of more than 300,000 convivial logophiles.

Grandiloquent means "pretentious or pompous in language, fashion, or behavior, especially in an extravagant way that's meant to impress." The words come from a variety of old, long-out-of-print dictionaries and glossaries of regional dialects. They fall typically into three basic categories:

- *delightfully obscure words that sound silly or have highly relatable meanings*
- *pompous terms that aren't obscure—because grandiloquent doesn't mean obscure and vice versa—for the edification of younger readers, courageous students of English as a second language, and anyone otherwise unfamiliar with the words*
- *antiquated slang that overlaps somehow with the first two categories*

Some argue that grandiloquent words, arcane and abstruse in nature, have no real value or function in modern society. To those calumniators, I say: *piffle paffle!* The more words you know, the more tools you have to articulate accurately the world, the people around you, your experiences, and the way you feel. Good and effective communication demands precision, so using the right words, grandiloquent or otherwise, matters. Others take perverse pleasure in vaunting their grandiose vocabulary, whether to veil some shady skulduggery or to inflate their social standing, usually by making the rest of us feel small. It therefore behooves us to kick that inflated linguistic pedestal from under those bloviators by arming ourselves with an equally sesquipedalian lexicon. De-snob the snobs by out-sesquipedalianizing them, say I!

Grandiloquent *mots justes* impart invaluable verisimilitude to reenactments, historical festivals, and cons. Grant your cosplay or LARPing the gravitas it deserves! Words such as *valetudinarian, ultracrepidarian,* or *floccinaucinihilipilification* also can derail (some of) those meetings that should've been emails. Speaking of meetings and emails, your newfound mellifluous loquacity will declare unmistakably to the entire office that you are a bona fide smarty-pants entirely worthy of a raise, promotion, cushy corner office with a view, your own parking space, a company credit card, more time off, and a juicy bonus.

By no means is this book meant to serve as an exhaustive, scholarly reference. Use it as a lodestar on your quest for linguistic dexterity and don't be afraid, should the need for further clarification arise, to augment the information provided here with the aid of a certain ubiquitous search engine. Herein, you'll find basic phonetic pronunciations for the words. I've eschewed the International Phonetic Alphabet (a less tasty IPA) for the simple reason that not everyone, particularly younger readers, knows or understands its technical intricacies. The basic phonetic approximations will land you in the ballpark, which is close enough because pronunciations vary from one region to the next, as of course they should. This book also makes use of a time-honored tradition called Grangerism: sourcing pictures from other books to illustrate one's own. All the illustrations come from publications that have fallen into the public domain.

Read the words in whatever order you like, but indulge my ever-so-gentle nudging for you to read it in order, cover to cover. However you approach it, you'll discover a trove of words suitable for every aspect of life, from the sacred to the profane, from the mundane to the celebratory, and everything between—including some words for which anyone possessing, shall we say, delicate sensibilities should consider a girding of the loins. Enjoy this book, dear reader, as the act of amusement and elucidation it is intended to be. Prithee, be not agitated by the above-average abundance of artful alliteration nor the prose which at times appears as perfectly purple as a plum picked in the prime of its pulchritudinous plumpness.

I

MUNDANE MORPHEMES

(EVERYDAY WORDS)

COWSLEM

(also: Causlem)

KOWZ-luhm,
KAHZ-luhm

noun

An ancient name for the evening star.

From Scots *cow*, from Old English *cū* + *leam* (gleam, flash of light), from Old Scots *leme* (brightness, radiance), from Old English *leoma* (ray, beam of light).

"When she awoke she found it was sunset; the welkin was tinged by a variety of colours which seemed to die away into an endless variety of fantastic forms, the perspective of each, beautifully tinged with the mild silvery light of Causlem (the name of the evening star) and all rapidly disappearing in the encreasing splendour of the Queen of Heaven."

—THOMAS WILKIE,
Proceedings of the Berwickshire Naturalists' Club, 1830

Spending the night engaged in astromantic study of the **cowslem** *and other celestial bodies has given Lady Verbena Vellwyn invaluable insight into the future.*

OSCITANCY

AH-sih-tuhn-see

noun

Great fatigue or sluggishness marked by pandiculation and dullness of wit.

From Latin *oscitans* (yawning), from *os* (mouth) + *citare* (to move, to put in motion) + *-y*, from Latin *-ia* (suffix of abstraction), from Ancient Greek *-ία* (*-ia*).

"It is not an ambition, that can be gratified by the distribution of places and pensions. This is a passion, that can only dwell in the weakest and most imbecil minds. Its necessary concomitants, are official inattention and oscitancy."

—WILLIAM GODWIN, *Four Early Pamphlets*, circa 1783

*Dayspring awakens avian melodies, heralding the dawn, as **oscitancy** overtakes the cultured clairvoyant who cavalierly eschewed slumber-tide.*

DAWLESS

(also: dowless)

DAH-luhss

adjective

Lazy, inactive, destitute of energy.

From dow, from Middle English *douen*, from Old English *dugan* (to have strength) + -less, from Middle English *-les*, from Old English *lēas* (lacking, loose from, false).

"An' a' that rackt Tam's curly pow Was gif Dod Broon wad keep his vow . . . Or swither like a dowless fule."

—JOHN HORNE, *Lan'wart Loon*, 1928

*The **dawless** demoiselle collects her accoutrements and brings them inside before answering the soporose call of the ethereal berceuse gamboling through her mind.*

4

YAWMAGORP

YAH-muh-gohrp

noun

A lounging idler who yawns, gapes, and stretches.

Regional: Leicestershire. From yawm, variant of yawn, from Middle English *yanen* (to yawn), from Old English *ginian* or *ganian* (to yawn, to gape) + gorp (mouth), perhaps from Middle English *gapen*, from Old Norse *gapa* (to gape).

"He's got a fit o't yawmagorps."

—SIDNEY OLDALL ADDY,
*A Glossary of Words Used in the Neighbourhood of Sheffield,
Including a Selection of Local Names and Some Notices
of Folk-lore, Games, and Customs,* 1888

Reduced to a limp, lethargic **yawmagorp**, *she scrides toward the tantalizing bed,
which somehow seems perpetually just beyond reach.*

SNERDLE

SNUHR-duhl

verb

1. **To nestle closely.**

2. **To wrap up pleasantly in bed.**

3. **To fall comfortably asleep.**

Regional: Nottinghamshire. Origin unknown.

"Maybe Felicia was one of a crack team of con artists who traveled around the city picking out likely chumps, confusing them with a foreign language, softening their hearts with pathetic tales, snerdling into their homes."

—LAURA FLAHERTY, "The Woman in Pink,"
Chicago Reader, 1988

*After a chasmal galpening, the affluent astrologess **snerdles** into the soft, warm covers and surrenders herself to the comforting arms of Morpheus.*

TINTINNABULATION

tin-tih-NAB-yoo-LAY-shuhn

noun

A tinkly, ringing, or jingly sound.

From "The Bells" by Edgar Allan Poe, from Latin *tintinnabulum* (bell), from *tintinnare* (to ring, to jingle) + -ation, from Latin -*atio*, variant of -*tio* (nominative suffix).

"Across the darkling meadows, from the heights of Hare, the tintinnabulation sounded mournfully, penetrating the curl-wreathed tympanums of Lady Parvula de Panzoust."

—RONALD FIRBANK, *Valmouth*, 1919

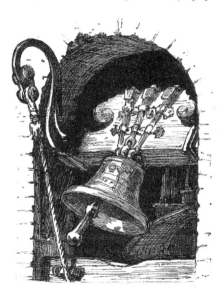

*Roused by the tuneful **tintinnabulation** of a telegraphic transmission, the mystic mondain opens one eye to peer from a ponderous perch of pillows.*

ROUKY

(also: rowky)

ROO-kee

adjective

Misty or foggy.

Regional: Scotland. From Scots *rouk* (mist, sea fog), perhaps from or influenced by Old Norse *rauk* (smoke, vapor), Old Frankish *rouc* (smoke), or Dutch *rook* (smoke).

"O! Blae was the mornin', an' rouky an' raw,
An' cauld blew the North wind, an' thick fell the snaw,
Whan an honest auld Souter set out frae his biel',
On a Visit o' business to H—r M'N—l."

—EBENEZER PICKEN, "The Visit," from
Miscellaneous Poems, Songs, etc. Partly in the Scottish Dialect, 1818

*A hushed and **rouky** morningtide lies shimmering like silver dust outside the picture window, calling to mind the fabled brume of Avalon.*

PANDICULATE

pan-DIK-yoo-layt

verb

To stretch as when newly awake, usually in conjunction with yawning.

From Latin *pandiculari* (to stretch oneself), from *pandere* (to stretch).

"Moreover, the intellect of the said examples being equal to their pulchritude, they relax, they pandiculate their members, they rest their bodies, they quietly play micating their digits, while my said Lord meditates; and, at his supernal signal, by the aid of the chalked carpet, they reproduce themselves in the accurate position wherein they had been collocated."

—FREDERICK WILLIAM ROLFE,
Don Renato: An Ideal Content, 1909

Pandiculating upward with arms akimbo, the soothsaying aristocrat feels an exigent need for coffee, the preferred prowess-providing potion for pulchritudinous pythonesses.

9

GALPEN

GAHL-*puhn*
verb

1. To gape, to yawn.

2. To yelp.

From Middle English *galp*, from Middle Dutch *galpen* (to yelp, to bark like a fox), from West Flemish *galpen* (to laugh rudely).

"And with a galpyng mouth hem alle he keste,
And seyde that it was tyme to lye adoun."

—GEOFFREY CHAUCER, *The Canterbury Tales*, circa 1395

*Stretching and **galpening** once more with an eldritch caterwaul, she waits patiently for the dark magic brew to endow its enlivening ensorcellment.*

SCURRYFUNGE

SKUHR-ee-funj

verb

To rush around the house in a mad cleaning spree after learning that a visitor is coming.

Perhaps from Middle English *scurry* (to rush or move hastily) + Latin *fungi* (to perform, execute, or complete, as with a task).

"Two of the brushes above-said must be for inside scurryfunging, viz., they must be hooked."

—William Cowper, "Letter to Lady Hesketh," 1789

*A perfunctory shufti about her disheveled drawing room reveals that, much to her ladyship's chagrin, she must needs undertake a **scurryfunge**.*

FOOFARAW

FOO-fuh-rah

noun

1. Inordinate fuss over insignificant piffle, much ado about nothing.

....

2. Garish decoration or ornamentation.

....

Regional: America. Perhaps from French *fanfaron* (boasting), from Spanish *fanfarrón*, from Arabic فَرْفَار (farfār).

"A kinship born . . . of a common humor, and a common liking for the kind of theatrical display which Andy contemptuously calls 'foofaraw.'"

—*NEW YORK TIMES BOOK REVIEW*, 1933

*A fleetfooted **foofaraw** ensues, with the customary throwing, scrubbing, and dusting.*
"Honestly, it's the only way these things ever get done around here," she sighs.

12

QUARION

KWAH-ree-uhn

noun

A cylinder or cube of wax or tallow with a central strip designed to emit light as it burns, a candle.

From quarrier (large square candle), perhaps from quarry (square shaped), from Middle English *quarrel* (square-shaped tile or stone), from Old French *quarel*, from Medieval Latin *quarellus* (paving stone, tile), from Latin *quadrum* (square), from *quattuor* (four) + *-ulus* (diminutive suffix).

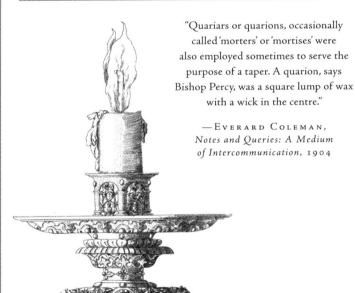

"Quariars or quarions, occasionally called 'morters' or 'mortises' were also employed sometimes to serve the purpose of a taper. A quarion, says Bishop Percy, was a square lump of wax with a wick in the centre."

—EVERARD COLEMAN,
Notes and Queries: A Medium of Intercommunication, 1904

The lady of the house clutches the coral-colored **quarion** *and carries it to its specified spot next to the baroque bronze pastille burner.*

SNAST

SNEIST

noun

A burned candlewick.

From Scots *snite* (to snuff a candle), from Old English *snÿtan* (to blow one's nose).

"Till some part of the Candle was consumed, and the Dust gathered about the Snast; But then it made the Snaste big, and long, and to burn duskishly."

—FRANCIS BACON, *Sylva Sylvarum*, 1626

Oh, these untidy **snasts** simply won't do at all, *she thinks while carefully trimming them to a more practical, pleasing measurement.*

FORFEX

FOHR-feks noun	**A pair of scissors.** From Latin *forfex* (shears).

"Fortunately for Belinda, 'the glittering forfex' was not immediately produced, as fine ladies do not now, as in former times, carry any such useless implements about with them."

—MARIA EDGEWORTH, *Belinda*, 1857

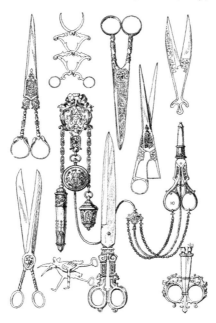

*In the top left drawer of the escritoire, she tucks the florid **forfex** neatly away, next to the pristinely polished pen nibs and the silver sealing wax.*

AUMBRY

AHM-bree noun	**A storage space—such as a pantry, cupboard, niche, locker, or chest—for utensils, vestments, or other objects.**

From French *ambry*, from Old French *almarie* (cupboard, bookcase, reliquary), from Latin *armarium* (closet, chest).

"Cromwell stepped to an aumbry, where there were a glass of wine, a manchet of bread, and a little salt."

—FORD MADOX FORD,
The Fifth Queen: And How She Came to Court, 1906

Half an hour flies by in a flash, and at last the sharpish chatelaine locks the door to the kitchen **aumbry** *with a satisfying click that punctuates her short-winded suspiration.*

WHIGMALEERIE

(also whigmaleery)

wig-muh-LEER-ee

noun

1. A trinket, knickknack, gimcrack, or geegaw; a flimsy but fanciful contrivance or ornament.

2. A fancy or whim.

Regional: Scotland. From Scots *figmaleery*, perhaps from Old Scots *fyke* (to fidget), from Old Norse *fíkjast* (to be eager or restless) + *ma* (interfix) + *leerie*, from Old Scots *lierie* (nonce word denoting sprightly motion or fanciful appearance).

"Just look at him, with an old taffeta whigmaleerie tied to his back, like Paddy from Cork, with his coat buttoned behind!"

—John Shaw Goldsmith,
The Shaving Shop, 1828

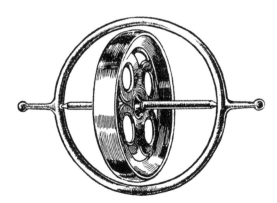

As a knock comes at the door, the now forswunk fraternizer espies an overlooked **whigmaleerie**; *a pert kick sends it darting under the dainty divan.*

SWAIBBLE

SWAY-buhl

verb

To mop, swab, or wash with vigor.

Regional: Scotland. From Scots *swabble*, perhaps influenced by Low German *swabbeln* (to splash from side to side).

"A've swaibblt masul weel up wui waeter."

—ELLIOT COWAN SMITH, *Braid Haaick*, 1927

*The scurryfunge complete, she opens the door to her coalesced comrades, flamboyantly directing them to her freshly **swaibbled** entrance with a flourish.*

DISCALCEATE

dis-KAL-see-ayt

verb

To remove one's shoes or sandals.

From Latin *discalceatus*, from *dis-* (prefix of removal) + *calceus* (shoe) + *-atus* (adjectival suffix).

"Such, among others, are the rites of discalceation, of investiture, of circumambulation, and of intrusting."

—ALBERT GALLATIN MACKEY, *The Symbolism of Freemasonry*, 1882

*The chatelaine kindly requests that her guests **discalceate** before entering the drawing room, its previously bemired surfaces swaibbled only just now.*

19

EMBRANGLEMENT

ehm-BRANG-guhl-mint

noun

1. A tricky or perplexing situation.

2. A long dispute or argument.

Regional: Leicestershire. From en- (in) + brangle, perhaps from French *branler* (to shake), from Old French *brandeler* (to agitate, to wave), from Latin *brandus* (firebrand, sword) + -ment, from Old French *-ment*, from Latin *-mentum* (suffix of result).

"During the highest fever of your interest in the fate of the royal Heroine . . . the constant distraction of your sympathies between her mental, and her corporeal, conflicts—the latter consisting of those restless fightings, kickings, and twitchings, in which the hands and feet of her dramatic Majesty are engaged, by the entanglements and embranglements of the latter, in her endless train."

—JAMES BERESFORD, *The Miseries of Human Life*, 1825

*Oswin Otterbuck, a consummate conservator, lugubriously relates a workplace **embranglement** at the museum involving one of the artists in residence eating his lunch . . . again.*

SWIVET

SWIH-viht,
SWIH-vuht

noun

1. An agitated state of mind; anxiety or panic.

2. A sense of urgency.

Regional: America. Origin unknown.

"Hilda, so Verity said, was in quite a swivit over
the prospect of being interviewed again."

—IRVIN COBB, *Murder Day by Day,* 1933

*The puerile prank of the purloined prandial has the choleric conservator in
something of a **swivet** as he pettishly picks at his brocade waistcoat.*

DOLORIFUGE

doh-LOHR-uh-fyooj

noun

Anything that alleviates feelings of sadness, loss, or disappointment, such as a hug, chocolate, or alcohol.

From Latin *dolor* (pain, grief) + *fugare* (to put to flight), from *fuga* (escape, exile).

"The children, who had made use of this idea of Tess being taken up by their wealthy kinsfolk (which they imagined the other family to be) as a species of dolorifuge after the death of the horse, began to cry at Tess's reluctance, and teased and reproached her for hesitating."

—THOMAS HARDY, *Tess of the d'Urbervilles,* 1891

Wanting to boost his spirits, famed fashionmonger Winter Westhaven, declares that the annoyed archivist needs a good old-fashioned **dolorifuge**.

GALLIMAUFRY

gal-uh-MAH-free

noun

1. A dish, especially a hash or ragout, made from various kinds of diced or minced meats.

2. Any absurd medley or hotchpotch.

From French *galimafrée* (hash), from Old French *calimafree* (meat stew). Further origins unknown, possibly from Old French *galer* (to enjoy) + Picard *mafrer* (to eat gluttonously).

"This so terrified Panurge that he forthwith said to Epistemon, The devil mince me into a gallimaufry if I do not tremble for fear!"

—FRANÇOIS RABELAIS, *Gargantua and Pantagruel*, translated by Thomas Urquhart, 1546/1693

*The restorer relates that his grandmama's **gallimaufry**, a cherished childhood comfort food, would be a deucedly delightsome dolorifuge indeed.*

RÉCHAUFFÉ

RAY-sho-FAY

noun

1. A dish of food warmed again.

2. Figuratively, something composed of old material, a rehash.

3. Leftovers.

From French *réchauffé* (reheated), from Latin *re-* (again) + Middle French *chaufer* (to warm), from Latin *calefacere* (to heat), from *calere* (to be warm) + *facere* (to make).

"The English groan for something better than the perpetual réchauffé of their literature."

—MARY OWENS CROWTHER, *How to Write Letters*, 1922

"Gallimaufry gladdens the gullet more the following day, when reheated and **réchauffé***," observes the culinarily contemplative conservator.*

HIRAETH

HEER-eith

noun

1. **A longing homesickness tinged with the loss of home and friendships vanished in time.**

2. **Yearning or regret.**

From Welsh *hiraeth* (longing), related to Cornish *hireth*, Old Irish *sírecht*, and Gaulish *siraxta*.

"Till death be pass'd, my love shall last,
My longing, my *hiraeth* for Wales."

—JOHN OWEN, *Gems of Welsh Melody*, 1860

Talk of his grandmama fills the pensive pedagogue with heart-felt **hiraeth** *as he reminisces about his childhood summers spent at Harville House in Tyverwyn-on-Sea.*

LEESOME

LEE-suhm adjective	**Pleasant, fair, or agreeable.** From Scots *leesome*, from Middle English *lefsum*, from Old English *léof* (dear, beloved) + *-sum* (suffix of similarity).

"A bonny leesome night, as e'er I saw:
The moon's as white's a new-blawn wreath o' snaw."

—GEORGE SMITH, *Douglas, a Tragedy in Five Acts by John Home,
Reduced to Scottish Rhyme, Chiefly in the Broad Buchan Dialect*, 1824

*Scanning the **leesome** light through the louvred lucarne, the blithesome band of
boulevardiers agree to egress and enjoy the fresh air and daystar while they last.*

BUMMEL

BUHM-uhl

noun, verb

1. A relaxing stroll.

2. To saunter in a relaxing manner; to amble, dawdle, or mosey.

From German *bummeln* (to stroll, to dilly-dally, to waver), from *bim-bam-bum*, iterative onomatopoeia for a bell ringing, related to *baumeln* (to dangle).

"It was the last evening of our Bummel; the early morning train would be the beginning of the end."

—Jerome K. Jerome, *Three Men on the Bummel*, 1900

*A balmy **bummel** through the leesome landscape sounds like a felicific idea, and everyone falls into high snuff in no time at all.*

CODDIWOMPLE

KAH-dee-
WAHM-puhl

verb, noun

1. To travel with a sense of purpose toward a vague destination as yet unknown.

2. The act of so traveling.

Slang, origin unknown.

"If you are anything like me you may be coddiwompling your way through life, which is not necessarily a bad thing. As long as you don't get catawampus in your coddiwomple, you're probably on the right track."

—DAVID BALLARD, "Don't Get Catawampus in Your Coddiwomple," PharosWealthStrategies.com, 2019

*As the congenial collective **coddiwomples** aimlessly onward, they discuss their vaticinated roles in the forthcoming fisticuffs against the sinister forces of the void—as one does.*

GROGGERY

GRAH-guhr-ee

noun

A disreputable drinking establishment or location, a dive bar or speakeasy.

From grog (alcohol diluted with water), named after Admiral Edward "Old Grog" Vernon, who wore a grogram coat, from French *gros* (coarse), from Medieval Latin *grossus* (large) + grain, from Old French *grain*, from Latin *granum* (seed) + Middle English *-erie*, from *-ier*, from *-er*, from Latin *-are* (infinitival suffix) + Middle English *-ie* (suffix of abstraction), from Latin *-ia*, from Ancient Greek *-ία* (*-ia*).

"They were passing a low groggery among the pines, when he came out of it, pistol in hand, and impudently ordered them to stop."

— MARTHA FINLEY, *Elsie's Vacation and After Events*, 1891

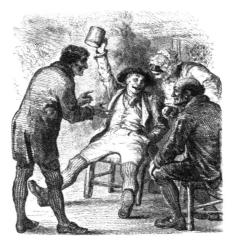

*After a gemütlich game of Lemur in the Gyre and some lackadaisical window-licking, the convivial coterie tucks into a glorified **groggery** to tipple and nosh.*

⇥ GALÈRE ⇤

gah-LEHR noun	**1. A group of objectionable people with a common interest, a rogues' gallery.**
	2. An unpleasant place or situation, a hassle.

From French *galère* (galley, oared ship), from Catalan *galera*, from Medieval Latin *galera*, from Byzantine Greek γαλέα (*galéa*), from Ancient Greek γαλεός (*galeós*: shark).

"'Why, your excellency,' he cried, in a tone of boundless surprise, 'what are you doing in this GALERE! All last evening I waited for you, at my house, and now—'"

—STANLEY WEYMAN,
From the Memoirs of a Minister of France, 1895

*The groggery's **galère** of goons engage in all manner of debauched divertissements, including cornhole, mahjong, and a spirited game of boulder, parchment, and forfex.*

HUBBLESHOO

HUH-buhl-shoo

noun

1. A confused throng of people.

2. A noisy uproar or disturbance.

Regional: Yorkshire. From Scots *hubbleshew* (uproar, mob), from Old Scots *hobillschowe*, from *hubble*, variant of Middle English *hobblen* + Scots *schow* (shove, attack), from Middle English *schoven*, from Old English *scūfan*.

"Da hubbleshue o' oot door wark tak's a' his time."

— GEORGE STEWART, *Shetland Fireside Tales*, 1877

*The door closes with a startling thump, and the harum-scarum **hubbleshoo** gawps like gongoozling gobemouches at the incongruous interlopers.*

31

GROAK

(also: growk)

GROHK

verb

To stare silently and intently at someone eating, hoping the eater will share some food; a habitude of every domestic canine ever to live.

From Scots *growk* (to look longingly).

"Nathan was stanin' at the table as uswal, growk-growkin' awa' for a bit o' my tea biskit."

—J. B. SALMOND, *My Man Sandy*, 1894

*While lamenting the low-rent luncheon, Winter Westhaven claps peepers on a fruesome chap who won't stop **groaking**.*

SUFFONSIFIED

(also: sophonsified)
suh-FAHN-sih-feid
adjective

Feeling content at the end of a meal, having eaten neither too much nor too little.

Regional: Canada. Origin unknown, perhaps from sufficient + satisfied.

"No, thank you, ma'am. My sufficiency has been suffonsified; any more would be obnoxious to my fastidious taste."

—Heidi Thomas, *Follow the Dream*, 2014

*The insufferably insipid comestibles leave no one sufficiently **suffonsified**, but neither can it be said that any of them angling for additional aliment.*

ABSQUATULATE

ab-SKWAH-choo-layt

verb

To leave or decamp abruptly.

Regional: America. From abscond (to leave hurriedly and secretly) + squattle (to depart) + ambulate (to walk), intended to resemble Latin.

"'But now,' went on the little old gentleman, 'we must all absquatulate.' He took her hand. 'Oh, must you?' she asked regretfully."

—ELEANOR GATES, *The Poor Little Rich Girl*, 1912

*The grotty groaker creeps increasingly closer, whereupon the fashionmonger decides to **absquatulate**, promptly paying the bill and exhorting the faction to festinate.*

RAMBALEUGH

(also: rumballiach)

RAM-buh-loo

adjective

Tempestuous or stormy.

Regional: Scotland. From Scots *ram-* (prefix of intensification), from English slang rum (excellent, fine, great), perhaps from Romani *rom* (husband, man) + *rumbullion* (tumult, uproar).

"Sic a rambaleugh nicht as this."

—A. J. B. PATERSON, *Mist from Yarrow*, 1900

*Outside the gruesome groggery, the air has grown unseasonably blustery, and the evening sky has become rambunctiously **rambaleugh**.*

WILLIWAW

WIL-ih-wah

noun

1. A cold gust of wind.

2. A whirlwind or squall.

Perhaps from willy (sudden squall), perhaps a variant of whirly, from whirl, from Middle English *whirlen*, from Old English *hweorfan* (to turn) + -y, from Old English -*ig* (qualitative suffix) + waw (a wave), perhaps from waff (gust or blast of air).

"'It's a williwaw!' adds the old sealer, in joyous tone, though at any other time, in open boat, or even decked ship, it would have sent a thrill of fear through his heart."

—CAPTAIN MAYNE REID, *The Land of Fire*, 1883

*The day's soothing psithurism yields to a wailing **williwaw** tearing through the streets, prompting a newspaper vendor to give chase to a tumult of unsecured publications.*

STERNUTATION

STUR-nyoo-TAY-shun

noun

A sneeze or the act of sneezing.

From Latin *sternutatio* (a sneeze), from *sternuere* (to sneeze) + *-tio* (nominative suffix).

"Would anyone believe that a simple sternutation could produce such ravages on a quadrupedal organism?"

— Gustave Flaubert,
Madame Bovary, translated by Eleanor Marx, 1856

*The worrisome williwaw triggers a sturt of **sternutation** for Mx. Winter Westhaven, who extracts a rose rococo kerchief with which to tend their perturbed proboscis.*

VICAMBULATE

vih-KAM-byoo-layt verb	**To walk along the streets and boulevards.** From Latin *vicus* (village) + *ambulare* (to walk).

"Many strangers were there among them, as Musical
Willie, who vicambulated greatly, soon perceived."

—MORTIMER COLLINS, *Squire Silchester's Whim, volume 2,* 1873

*The conservator vociferates over the aeolian howl that the crosswinds are
curtailing the coterie's capability to **vicambulate** through town.*

BUMBERSHOOT

BUM-bur-shoot

noun

A collapsible canopy, usually black, wielded against the rain; an umbrella.

Regional: America. From umbrella, from Latin *umbra* (shadow) + parachute, "chute," from Old French *cheoite* (fallen), from Latin *cadere* (to fall).

"Pack up my outfit, Mollie darling, in the suitcase once again! Stow my sweater in the shawl strap with the bumbershoot and cane!"

—*New York Times*, 1909

*Lady Vellwyn ensconces herself in a doorway, the gloomy gale wantonly whipping her burgundy **bumbershoot**, as the rosy restorer summons a conveyance.*

TAXIMETER CABRIOLET

tak-ZIM-ih-tur
KAB-ree-o-LAY

noun

A motorized vehicle for hire, abbreviated to "taxicab."

From Medieval Latin *taxa* (charge, fee) + French *mètre*, from Latin *metrum*, from Ancient Greek μέτρον (*métron*: measure) + French *cabriolet* (convertible carriage pulled by one horse), from Latin *caper* (goat) + *-olus* suffix indicating youth.

"Outside the taximeter cabriolet ground into gear and wheezed off, followed a moment later by the clopping of the horse's hooves."

—JAY LAKE, *Mainspring*, 2008

*Not a moment too soon, a tansy-tinted **taximeter cabriolet** speeds through the rambaleugh eventide to bear the gallivanters to their declared destination.*

ATHENAEUM

ATH-uh-NAY-uhm

noun

1. A library or reading room.

2. A literary or scientific club.

From Latin *Athenaeum*, from Ancient Greek Ἀθηναῖον (*Athēnaîon*: temple or building sacred to Athena), from Ἀθήνη (Athénē: Athena) + -ιον (-*ion*, suffix of place).

"We went off to the Athenaeum which is well stored with books."

—ROBERT HEYWOOD, *A Journey to America in 1834*, 1919

*Striving to curtail his convivial clientele's exposure to the trying tempest, the mannerly motorist hews close to the **athenaeum** and opens the door for them.*

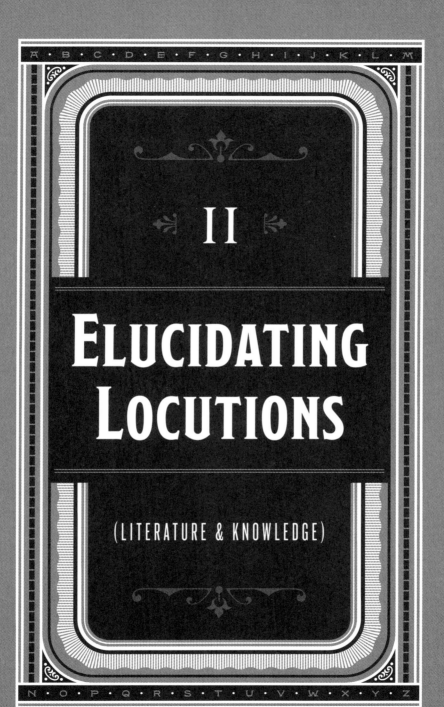

ELUCIDATING LOCUTIONS

(LITERATURE & KNOWLEDGE)

PHILOBIBLIAN

FIL-uh-BIB-lee-uhn

adjective

Enamored of books and literature.

From Latin *philobiblius* (book-loving), from Ancient Greek φίλος (*fílos:* dear, beloved) + βιβλίον (*biblíon:* paper, scroll).

"From these I proceeded gradually to higher branches of literature; and my method has since been to visit the philobiblian libraries, and other learned stalls, and the noble collections at Moorfields; in which choice repositories I have with infinite pleasure and advantage run over the elaborate systems of ancient divines, politicians, and philosophers, which have escaped the fury of pastry-cooks and trunk-makers."

—*The Connoisseur*, No. 86, 1755

Having survived the maelstrom, the **philobiblian** *friends stroll stylishly through the alabaster archway of the art deco athenaeum.*

OMNILEGENT

om-NIHL-ih-jent
adjective

Reading all things, addicted to reading.

From Latin *omni* (all) + *legens* (reader), from *legere* (to read).

"He was not exactly as Southey was, 'omnilegent'; but in his own departments, and they were numerous, he went farther below the surface and connected his readings together better than Southey did."

— George Saintsbury, *De Quincey*, 1890

A toplofty tazie precociously pronounces the bookish building a perfect place for **omnilegent** *personages to while away the hours.*

BIBLIOSOPH

BIB-lee-uh-SOHF noun	**One who cares for and maintains a library, a librarian.** From Ancient Greek βιβλίον (*biblíon*: paper, scroll) + σοφός (*sofós*: wise).

"At a desk under the stairway he saw a lean, studious, and kindly-looking bibliosoph, who was poring over an immense catalogue."

— CHRISTOPHER MORLEY, *The Haunted Bookshop*, 1919

*As the philobiblian friends enter the archive, Paige Penwiper, the beatific **bibliosoph** seated at the main desk, greets the group with a warm, sotto voce "Hello!"*

POLYHISTOR

pah-lee-HIS-tohr noun	**A well-educated individual, someone who has studied a wide variety of topics.**

From Ancient Greek πολύς (*polús*: many, much) + ἵστωρ (*hístor*: wise one).

"There are now none but Polyhistors who have read everything else, but not the ancients."

—JEAN PAUL, *The Invisible Lodge*, 1793

*The tousled trio greets the popular **polyhistor**, exchanging ceremonious salutations, which include a hugger-mugger handshake accompanied by a fleeting facial tick.*

CARRELL

(also: carrel)

KEHR-uhl

noun

A small desk or individual study area in a library.

From Medieval Latin *carula* (a small study in a cloister, an enclosure in which to read), from Latin *corolla* (little crown), from *corona* (garland, wreath) + *-la* (diminutive suffix).

"These carrels may be seen in unusual perfection in Gloucester."

—JULIA DE WOLF ADDISON,
Arts and Crafts in the Middle Ages, 1908

*Verbena Vellwyn entreats the lithesome librarian to rendezvous in a cozy little **carrell** to discuss a matter of great import.*

BIBLIOPHAGIST

bib-lee-AH-fuh-jist

noun

A passionate reader of books.

From Ancient Greek βιβλίον (*biblíon*: paper, scroll) + φάγος (*fágos*: eater, glutton), from φαγεῖν (*fageín*: to eat).

"That eminent bibliophagist, and printer of scarce tracts."

—*Sunday at Home, 1881*

*Remembering that the pulchritudinous pythoness long has delighted in the penumbra of the printed page, the lugubrious librarian smiles knowingly at her favorite **bibliophagist**.*

ARISTOPHRENIC

uh-RIS-toh-FREHN-ik,
AH-ris-toh-FREHN-ik

adjective

Possessing advanced intelligence.

From Ancient Greek ἄριστος (*áristos*: best) + φρήν
(*frén*: mind, spirit) + *-ic*, from Middle English *-ik*, from
Old French *-ique*, from Latin *-icus* (adjectival suffix).

Antonym: **CACOPHRENIC**

"My Lords, I thank my noble friend for that aristophrenic reply."

—NORMAN ST. JOHN-STEVAS,
"Lords Chamber: Cathedrals: Repair Funding," in
House of Lords Hansard, volume 513, column 741, 1989

*The brilliant bibliosoph considers the affluent astrologess one of the most **aristophrenic**
people she knows, a high compliment considering her own smarts and social circle.*

TANQUAM

TAHN-kwahm

noun

Someone sufficiently educated to attend college.

From Latin *tanquam socius* (just as a fellow), referring to anyone who is "just like a fellow" student of Cambridge University, from Latin *tam* (so) + *quam* (what, which).

"Thomas Dove, D.D. was born in this City, as a *credible person* of his nearest Relation hath informed me, bred a *Tanquam* (which is a *Fellowes Fellow*) in Pembroke-Hall in Cambridge."

—Tʜᴏᴍᴀs Fᴜʟʟᴇʀ, *The History of the Worthies of England*, 1662

The curious curatrix gushingly observes that the thouctish thaumaturge was a
tanquam *before the other children her age had begun grammar school.*

VADE MECUM

VAH-day MAY-koom

noun

1. A book or object that someone carries constantly.

2. A reference work that serves as an instruction manual or field guide, such as a cookbook, travel guide, or phrase book.

From Latin *vade* (go, walk [imperative]), from *vadere* (to go) + *me* (me) + *cum* (with) (in stylistic reversal).

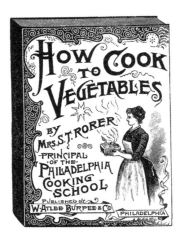

"Hereunto Pawruel very willingly consented, and they drank so neat that there was not so much as one poor drop left of two hundred and seven and thirty puncheons, except one boracho or leathern bottle of Tours which Panurge filled for himself, for he called that his vademecum, and some scurvy lees of wine in the bottom, which served him instead of vinegar."

—Fʀᴀɴçᴏɪꜱ Rᴀʙᴇʟᴀɪꜱ, *Gargantua and Pantagruel*, translated by Thomas Urquhart, 1546/1693

*The inheritress is searching for a rare reference, a **vade mecum** on vellum, and hopes that the administratrix of the athenaeum can help her find it.*

BOUQUINISTE

boo-kee-NEEST

noun

Someone who sells or deals in used or antique books.

From French *bouquin* (old book), from Middle Dutch *boec* (book), from West Germanic *bōk* + Middle Dutch *-inne* (diminutive suffix) + French *-iste*, from Latin *-ista*, from Ancient Greek -ιστής (*-istés*: suffix of agency).

"A library's ideal function is to be a little bit like a bouquiniste's stall, a place for trouvailles."

— UMBERTO ECO, *The Name of the Rose*, 1980

The bibliognost names someone who might be able to help: Baldavin Berggeist, the **bouquiniste** *of Braeburn Boulevard, who always sets old books aside for her.*

FACETIAE

fuh-SEE-she-ee

plural noun

Books of an objectionable kind, coarsely witty or indecent.

From Latin *facetiae* (jokes, cleverness), from *facetus* (witty) + *-ia* (suffix of abstraction), from Ancient Greek -ια (*-ia*).

"Why, now, there's a second-hand bookseller not a hundred miles from Holborn—and a pleasant, nice man he is, and does a respectable business—and he puts to the end of his catalogue—they all have catalogues that's in a good way—two pages that he calls 'Facetiae.' They're titles and prices of queer old books in all languages—indecent books, indeed."

—HENRY MAYHEW, *London Labour I, 1851*

*The cosmopolitan clairvoyant fanatically fancies fatuous **facetiae**, a jocund jouissance acquired at university, so she makes a mental note of the merchant's name.*

ENCHIRIDION

ehn-kih-RID-ee-uhn

noun

1. A book carried in the hand.

2. A manual or handbook.

From Ancient Greek ἐγχειρίδιον (*encheirídion*: held in the hand), from ἐν (*en*: in) + χείρ (*cheír*: hand) + -ίδιον (*-ídion*: diminutive suffix).

"I have been emboldened to present this small enchiridion . . . unto the hands and patronage of so . . . judicious a person."

—EDWARD REYNOLDS,
Meditations on the Holy Sacrament of the Lord's Last Supper, 1638

*Leaning into the librarian's confidence, the suave soothsayer reveals that, generations ago, the enshrined **enchiridion** was purloined from one of her progenitors.*

OPUSCULUM

uh-PUS-kyoo-luhm

noun

A minor literary work.

From Latin *opus* (labor, work) + *-culus* (diminutive suffix).

Antonym: **PANDECT**

"At least I desire his censure of this Opusculum, but newly hatched, may be but as milde, as my intentions reall for the more certain and speedy advancement of learning."

—SIMON DAINES, *Orthoepia Anglicana*, 1640

In hushed tones, she warns that the obscure object represents no ordinary **opusculum**, *no bush-league bagatelle; oh no, quite the contrary!*

PANDECT

PAN-dekt

noun

1. A universal dictionary or encyclopedia.

2. A comprehensive digest or treatise containing the whole of any science.

From Latin *pandectes* (encyclopedia), from Ancient Greek πανδέκτης (*pandéktēs*: all-receiver), from πᾶς (*pâs*: all) + δέκτης (*déktēs*: recipient).

Antonym: **OPUSCULUM**

"While the empire was possessed by the princes of the house of Saxony, a copy of the Pandects of Justinian was discovered at Amalfi."

— CHARLES BUTLER, *The Life of Hugo Grotius*, 1826

*At one time, this pantagruelian **pandect**, this titanic tome, lay enshrined deep in the secret archives of the Alumbrado, who had spirited it away and hid it from the world.*

BIBLIOTAPH

BIB-lee-uh-TAF

noun

Someone who hides or buries books or keeps them under lock and key.

From French *bibliotaphe*, from Ancient Greek βιβλίον (*biblíon*: paper, scroll) + τάφος (*táfos*: tomb, burial).

"The Bibliotaph was mightily pleased with both: the one, he said, appealed to him aesthetically, the other dietetically."

—LEON VINCENT, *The Bibliotaph and Other People*, 1898

The leesome librarian divulges a panoptic jealousy of anyone with access to the apocryphal archives of those most bureaucratic of **bibliotaphs.**

BOOKWRIGHT

BOOK-reit

noun

1. **A writer of books, an author (disparaging).**

2. **Someone who prints and binds books.**

From Middle English *bok*, from Old English *bōc* + Middle English *wrighte*, from Old English *wyrhta* (maker, worker).

"This is truly to be carnifex papiri, A murderer of paper, as Illyricus comonly calleth the Zuinglians, this is in deede to be miserabilis librifex, a miserable bookewright, as Luther malapertly nameth King Henry, a learned prince and of famous memory."

—WILLIAM RAINOLDS,
A Refutation of Sundry Reprehensions, 1583

*A sesquicentenary ago, a descendant of the original **bookwright** liberated the Vellwyn Vellum at great personal peril, reclaiming it for the alleged edification of his lineage.*

VOCULATION

vahk-yoo-LAY-shuhn

noun

The proper and correct pronunciation and enunciation of words.

From Latin *voculatio* (pronunciation), from *vox* (voice) + *-ula* (diminutive suffix) + *-tio* (nominative suffix).

"What is the universe to him, if not the one absolute vox inflecting itself into its involved voculations?"

—JAMES HUTCHISON STIRLING,
The Secret of Hegel, volume 2, 1865

*The beatific bibliosoph inquires whether, when reading aloud from the tome, the elocutionist particularly must heed the **voculation**, lest peril most grievous result.*

GALIMATIAS

gahl-ee-MAH-tee-uhs,
gahl-ee-MAY-she-uhs

noun

Academic nonsense, intellectual poppycock, or muddled, senseless blabbering.

From French *galimatias* (rigmarole, fuss, bother). Further origins unknown.

"Now it seemed to me that Mr. C—— had no opinions, only words, for his assertions seemed a mere galimatias."

—H. C. ROBINSON, *Diary, June 10th,* 1869

*Lady Vellwyn confirms that, to the uninitiated eye, the inscrutable text looks like a load of **galimatias**, so its orators must train to read it with meticulous precision.*

TRANTY

(also: trantie)
TRAN-tee

adjective

Wise above one's years, precocious, advanced; often used to describe children.

Regional: Scotland. From Middle English *trant* (trickery, cunning), from Middle Dutch *trant* (a step), from *tranten* (to walk) + *-y*, from Old English *-ig* (qualitative suffix).

"About this period died at Hawick two lone sisters . . . designated the Tranties, rather more intelligent than their neighbours in a similar humble condition of life."

—JAMES WILSON, *Hawick and Its Old Memories*, 1858

*The leery librarian considers the pulchritudinous pythoness a **tranty** lass, but does she truly desire the burden of responsibility that comes with ownership of such a volume?*

ELUCUBRATE

eh-LOO-koo-brayt,
eh-LOO-kyoo-brayt

verb

To write or work by candlelight.

From Latin *elucubrare* (to write or compose by lamplight), from *ex-* (out of) + *lucubro* (night work by candlelight) from *lux* (light).

"The result was a long dramatic elucubration, which reminds us involuntarily of certain of Mlle. Smith's subliminal productions"

—MICHAEL SAGE, *Mrs. Piper & the Society for Psychical Research,* 1904

Encumbered evading evildoers, the affluent astrologess wonders why her progenitor ever endeavored to **elucubrate** *such a ghastly tome.*

CUGGER-MUGGER

KUH-gur-MUH-gur
noun

A clandestine conversation; whispered gossip.

Origin unknown, perhaps from Irish *cogar* (whisper) + Old Norse *mjúkr* (meek, soft) or Victorian rhyming slang, related to Scots *cuddle-muddle* (to speak in secret).

"There was a great laugh at Tim's answer; and then there was a whispering, and a great cugger mugger, and coshering."

—THOMAS CROFTON CROKER,
Fairy Legends and Traditions of the South of Ireland, 1859

The thouchtish thaumaturge shares the **cugger-mugger** *that the volume imparts unfathomable power that puts one's soul, indeed everyone's soul, in the greatest peril.*

ULTRACREPIDARIAN

UHL-truh-KREP-ih-DEHR-ee-uhn

noun, adjective

1. **A know-it-all who gives opinions on topics beyond one's knowledge.**

2. **Pertaining to someone who talks about matters beyond the scope of one's knowledge.**

From the Latin phrase *sutor ne ultra crepidam* (the cobbler no further than his shoes), from *ultra* (beyond) + *crepida* (sandal), from Ancient Greek κρηπίς *(krēpís)* + Latin *-arius* (suffix of agency) +*-anus* (adjectival suffix).

"The last sort I shall mention are *verbal critics*—mere word-catchers, fellows that pick out a word in a sentence and a sentence in a volume, and tell you it is wrong. (The title of *Ultra-Crepidarian critics* has been given to a variety of this species.)"

—WILLIAM HAZLITT,
Table-Talk Volume 2, 1822

*No blathering **ultracrepidarian** herself, the docent trusts the insightful inheritress and forthwith arranges an introduction to the benevolent bouquiniste.*

HELLUO LIBRORUM

HEL-yoo-oh
lih-BROH-ruhm

noun

Someone with an insatiable appetite for reading books, a bookworm.

From Latin *helluo librorum* (glutton for books).

"One of these brothers was called Comestor . . . as it were booke-eater,
because he was such a Helluo librorum, a devourer of bookes."

—SIMON BIRCKBEK, *The Protestants Evidence*, 1635

*The auguring heiress must lay hands on the book before some hapless **helluo librorum**
lays hands on it, thrusting everyone into a seriously sticky wicket.*

LEXIPHANIC

LEK-sih-FAN-ik
adjective

Linguistically bombastic, inflated, pretentious, or turgid.

From Λεξιφάνης (*Lexiphánes*), a satire by Λουκιανὸς ὁ Σαμοσατεύς (Lucian of Samosata), from Ancient Greek λέξις (*léxis*: speech, diction) + φαίνειν (*faínein*: to show, to make visible).

"I generally found them [modern writings] more or less Lexiphanick in proportion to the share of fame and reputation their several authors enjoyed."

—ARCHIBALD CAMPBELL, *Lexiphanes, a Dialogue*, 1767

The levelheaded librarian discloses that the bookseller has an impish tendency to spout **lexiphanic** *around those he meets for the first time.*

EUPHUISM

YOO-*fyoo-IZ-uhm*,
YOO-*foo-IZ-uhm*

noun

An affected style in speech or writing, originating in the 1500s, characterized by alliteration, consonance, a wide vocabulary, verbal antithesis, and odd combinations of words.

From *Euphues: The Anatomy of Wit* by John Lyly, from Ancient Greek εὐφυής (*euphuēs*: witty, graceful) from εὐ- (*eu-*: good) + φυή (*fué*: stature) + -ism, from Ancient Greek -ισμός (*-ismós*: suffix of abstraction).

"Her advances had been met with coldness, and 'something more;' her perfumed little notes, written in a style of euphuism all her own, had been left unanswered; her presents of fruit and flowers unacknowledged."

— CHARLES LEVER, *The Daltons*, volume 1, 1852

*Fans of verbal frippery, Lady Vellwyn's cadre indulges in more than a little **euphuism**, so she and the bookseller doubtlessly will get along like toast and marmalade.*

SCIOLISM

SY-uh-LIZ-uhm

noun

1. The pretense of having a deeper understanding of a topic about which one has only a shallow understanding.

2. The spouting of opinions on topics beyond one's knowledge.

3. Superficial or shallow knowledge.

From Medieval Latin *sciolus* (smatterer), from Latin *scius* (knowing, cognizant) + *-olus* (diminutive suffix) + -ism, from Ancient Greek -ισμός (*-ismós*: suffix of abstraction).

"It is probable, indeed, that such of the former, as mistake sciolism for philosophy, must have consequently often mistaken the trivial for the important in these researches."

—*The Monthly Review*, volume 8, 1753

*The bewitching bibliognost knows that the bookseller doesn't suffer **sciolism** on anyone's part, calling it out the instant he catches wind of any supercilious poppycock.*

PHILOSOPHASTER

fih-LAH-sih-FAS-tuhr

noun

A pretender to philosophical knowledge, an impostor philosopher, a philosophe.

From Latin *philosophaster* (a dabbler in philosophy), from *philosophus*, from Ancient Greek φίλος (*filos*: dear, beloved) + σοφός (*sofós*: wise) + Latin *-aster* (suffix of incompleteness or shortcoming).

"It has furnished an axiomatic foundation for the philosophy of philosophasters and for the moralizing of sentimentalists."

—THOMAS HENRY HUXLEY, *Evolution and Ethics*, 1893

The bonhomous book merchant has a fondness for Grandiloquent Words, *but he's no common* **philosophaster** *prone to interminable maundering or punctilious yammering.*

SOPHOMANIAC

SAH-foh-MAY-nee-ak
noun

A person possessing the delusion of superior intelligence.

From Ancient Greek σοφός (*sofós*: wise) + μανία (*manía*: madness) + -ac, from French -*acque*, from Latin -*acus*, from Ancient Greek -ακός (-*akós*: qualitative suffix).

"Don't waste your time arguing with sophomaniacs. It is far better to ignore them completely, or poke them in the eye."

—PETER NOVOBATZKY AND AMMON SHEA,
Depraved and Insulting English, 2001

*The bouquiniste has developed a sensitivity to **sophomaniacs**, philosophasters, and poseurs, but he remains resolutely willing to help them lighten their purses.*

CACOPHRENIC

kah-koh-FREHN-ik

adjective

Pertaining to a dysfunctional mind or inferior intellect.

From Ancient Greek κακός (*kakós*: bad) + φρήν (*frén*: mind, spirit) + -ic, from Middle English *-ik*, from Old French *-ique*, from Latin *-icus* (adjectival suffix).

Antonym: **ARISTOPHRENIC**

"Two of the zipsuited chims' faces bore the stigmata of failed genetic meddling—mottled, cacophrenic features or the blinking, forever-puzzled look of a cross-wired brain—embarrassing reminders that Uplift was an awkward process, not without its price."

—DAVID BRIN, *The Uplift War*, 1995

*The majority of his clientele consists of **cacophrenic** aristocrats looking to bolster their bookshelves merely to impress their minions and mistresses.*

LEXICOMANE

LEK-sih-coh-mahn

noun

A person who loves dictionaries.

From Ancient Greek λεξικός (*lexikós*: pertaining to words), from λέξις (*léxis*: saying, speech), from λέγειν (*légein*: to speak) + French *-mane* (suffix describing mania), from Ancient Greek -μανής (*-manés*), from μανία (*manía*: madness).

"Those lexicomanes will, no doubt, prefer to disregard the recent study that links the preference for long words and jargon with feelings of insecurity rather than intellectual prowess."

— from "Why Sesquipedalian Loquaciousness?,"
Economic Times, 2020

*The beneficent bookseller has a particular place in his heart for **lexicomanes**, counting his diehard dedication a billet-doux to those purest of logophiles.*

III

BEEF-WITTED BLATTEROONS

(INSULTS & ANTONYMS)

MYRMIDON

MUR-mih-dahn

noun

A blindly devoted and unquestioning follower, someone who executes commands unscrupulously.

From Latin *Myrmidones*, from Ancient Greek Μυρμιδόνες (*Murmidónes*: warriors led by Achilles to Troy). Not related, as believed in the early Roman Empire, to μυρμηδών (*murmēdón*: ant nest), from μύρμηξ (*múrmēx*: ant).

Antonym: FUGLEMAN

FYOO-guhl-muhn

noun

Someone who takes initiative, setting an example for others to follow, particularly a leader or ringleader.

From flugleman, from German *flügel* (wing) + *mann* (man).

"The Southern who harried their glens with his canine myrmidons in the evil days ere King Jamie annexed England to Scotland."

—W. H. RUSSELL,
My Diary in India, 1860

*After innumerable inquiries, Baldavin Berggeist confirms that a malicious **myrmidon** in the service of Lord Greensquire also is seeking the book.*

DUNDERWHELP

DUHN-duhr-wehlp

noun

A foolish, slow-witted imbecile.

From dunder, perhaps from Dutch *donder* (thunder), from Middle Dutch *donre* + whelp (puppy, wolf cub), from Middle English *whelp*, from Old English *hwelp*.

Antonymous: **SONSY**

SAHN-zee,
SAHN-see

adjective

1. Lucky.

2. Happy, good-humored.

3. Well-conditioned, buxom.

From sonse (abundance, prosperity, happiness, luck), from Scots *sonasach*, from Gaelic *sonas* (good fortune, happiness) + *-y*, from Old English *-ig* (qualitative suffix).

"What a purblinde Puppy was I; now I remember him.
All the whole cast on's face, though 'twere umber'd,
And mask'd with patches: what a dunder-whelp
To let him domineer thus: how he strutted,
And what a load of Lord he clapt upon him!"

—JOHN FLETCHER,
The Wild Goose Chase, 1621

*A duplicitous **dunderwhelp**, the ham-fisted henchman has rough edges but familial ties to the Knights of Pétomane, which has afforded to him certain advantages in life.*

GIMCRACK

(also: jimcrack) *JIM-krak* adjective	**Ostentatious but worthless; gaudy or gimmicky.** From Middle English *gibecrake*, perhaps from Middle English *gibben* (to waver), from Old French *giber* (to shake) + crack, from Middle English *crakken*, from Old English *cracian* (to crack, to resound).

Antonymous: **TATTERDEMALION**

TA-tuhr-duh- *MAL-ee-uhn* adjective, noun	**1. Disheveled, tattered, torn.** **2. Someone wearing such clothing, a ragamuffin.** Reduced from tatterdemallion, from tatter, from Middle English *tatered*, from Old Norse *toturr* + French *de* (preposition of origin), from Latin *de* + French *maillot* (shirt), from Old French *mailloel*, from *maille* (chainmail), from Latin *macula* (mesh, hole, cell).

"You are now (thanks to Mr. Whitbread)
got into a large, comfortable house.
Not into a gimcrack-palace; not into
a Solomon's temple; not into a frost-
work of Brobdignag filigree; but into
a plain, honest, homely, industrious,
wholesome, brown brick playhouse."

—HORACE SMITH AND JAMES
SMITH, "In the Character of a Hampshire
Farmer," *Rejected Addresses*, 1812

*A **gimcrack** fellow with all the hollow frippery of the aristocracy, Lord Greensquire possesses
more pounds than perspicacity, as is generally the case with those of his station.*

FLAMFOO

FLAM-foo

noun

1. A gaudily dressed woman.

2. A gaudy ornament of female dress.

Regional: Scotland. From flamfew (moonlight reflected on water, a gewgaw, something fantastic), perhaps from Old French *fanfelue* (trifle), from Medieval Latin *famfaluca* (bubble, lie), from Ancient Greek πομφόλυξ (*pomfólux*: air bubble).

Antonym: BROOKSY

BROOK-see

noun

An elegant, fashionable dresser.

From 1920s flapper slang Joe Brooks (a dapper, well-dressed man), from average Joe (generic name for a man) + Brooks Brothers (apparel company) + -y from Old English -*ig* (diminutive suffix).

"It was sheerly impossible that the jocular mood of my host should have blossomed into this manifestation, but there was something to be said for the theory, that Fancy grown licorous and freakish on the lush undergrowths of an imagination always in a slight degree morbid, had bodied forth a curious flamfew."

— from "Stanley Rippenger's Recital:
A Romance of Modern Life,"
*Temple Bar: A London Magazine for
Town and Country Readers*, 1890

*With his penchant for bombastic ballyhoo, Lord Greensquire insists that his noble wife
attire herself in the hilarious habiliments of a farcical* **flamfoo**.

TAZIE

TAY-zee

noun

1. A fit of passion, a struggle, or a tussle.

2. A romping, foolish girl.

Regional: Scotland. From Scots *tazie* (diminutive of tease), from Old English *tæsan* (to tease).

Antonym: MRS. GRUNDY

MIS-iz GRUHN-dee

noun

Someone who prudishly adheres to conventional propriety, a stick-in-the-mud.

From "Mrs. Grundy," a character in *Speed the Plough* by Thomas Morton.

"For poets are in love right crazy,
An' up Parnassus, wi' a tazie,
Ye'll leg, an' lean."

—ANDREW SCOTT,
Poems, 1805

The predatory paparazzi, myrmidons all, sell photos of Lady Greensquire that make her appear to be frolicking about like some kind of tittivated, tittering **tazie.**

APISTIA

ah-pis-TEE-uh

noun

Unfaithfulness, particularly in matters of religion or marriage.

From Ancient Greek ἀπιστία (*apistía*: unbelief, faithlessness), from ἀ- (*a-*: without) + πίστις (*pístis*: faith).

Antonym: HEREISM

HEER-iz-uhm

noun

Marital fidelity.

From Middle English *hēr*, from Old English *hēr* (at this place) + -ism, from Ancient Greek -ισμός (*-ismós*: suffix of abstraction).

"Johann was a sly and crafty fellow: having inserted a clause in his prenuptial agreement asserting that apistia could not be considered grounds for alimony, he now was free to whore his way about town with complete abandon."

—PETER NOVOBATZKY AND AMMON SHEA, *Depraved English*, 1999

*One daily rag recounted the baron's indelicate **apistia** with the scullery maid and the chauffeur while the midwife was tending to the birthing baroness.*

IMBONITY

ihm-BOH-nih-tee

noun

A lack of goodness.

From Latin *imbonitas* (insolence, contemptuousness), from *im-* (not) + *bonitas* (goodness), from *bonus* (good, honest) + *-itas* (nominative suffix).

Antonym: KALOKAGATHIA

KAH-lo-kah-GAH-thee-uh,
KAH-lo-kah-GAY-thee-uh

noun

1. A character marked by goodness and honor.

2. The balanced unity of moral, physical, and spiritual virtues.

From Ancient Greek καλοκαγαθία (*kalokagathía*: goodness, nobility), from καλοκάγαθος (*kalokágathos*: gentleman), from καλός καὶ ἀγαθός (*kalós kaì agathós*: beautiful and good) + -ία (*-ía*: suffix of abstraction).

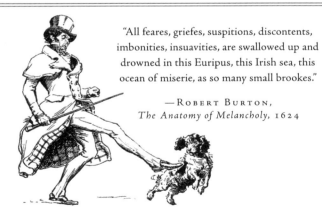

"All feares, griefes, suspitions, discontents, imbonities, insuavities, are swallowed up and drowned in this Euripus, this Irish sea, this ocean of miserie, as so many small brookes."

—ROBERT BURTON,
The Anatomy of Melancholy, 1624

Odious acts of ignoble **imbonity** *always catch up to repugnant reprobates who dissolutely disrespect their helpmeets in such flagrant fashion.*

GANDERMOONER

GAN-*duhr*-MOO-*nuhr*

noun

A husband who pursues other women while his wife is pregnant and for a period after she gives birth.

From Middle English *gander* (male goose), from Old English *gandra* + Middle English *mone* (moon), from Old English *mona* + -er, from Old English -ere, perhaps from Latin -arius (suffix of agency).

Antonymous: UXORIOUS

uhk-ZOHR-ee-uhs,
ook-ZOHR-ee-uhs,

adjective

Inordinately attentive to one's wife to the point of obsequious submission.

From Latin *uxorius* (wifely), from *uxor* (wife) + -ius (adjectival suffix), from Old Latin -ios.

"What'er we get by gulls
Of country or of city,
Old flat-caps or young heirs,
Or lawyers' clerks so witty;
By sailors newly landed,
To put in for fresh waters;
By wandering gander-mooners,
Or muffled late-night walkers,
With a hone, etc."

—THOMAS MIDDLETON,
A Fair Quarrel, 1617

With the gallivanting **gandermooner's** *sights set on her book, Verbena Vellwyn intends to reclaim it before the bumptious baron's heinous henchman can put his paws on it.*

WALLYDRAIGLE

WAH-lee-DREH-guh noun	**A small, frail, or feeble person.**

Regional: Scotland. From Scots *wallydrag*, from Old Scots *walidrag*, from *waly* (exclamation of sorrow), perhaps reduced from *walawa*, from Old Scots *wallawa* + Scots *draigle* (dirty, untidy person).

Antonymous: **PUISSANT**

PWIS-uhnt, *PWEE-suhnt* adjective	**Authoritative, mighty, powerful.**

From Middle English *puissaunt*, from Middle French *puissant*, from Old French *pussant*, from *pooir* (to be able), from Latin *posse*.

"That canna be said o' king's soldiers, if they let themselves be beaten wi' a wheen auld carles that are past fighting . . . and wives wi' their rocks and distaffs, the very wally-draigles o' the countryside."

—WALTER SCOTT,
Rob Roy, 1817

*A guileful, wileful **wallydraigle**, the namby-pamby nobleman has unseemly ambitions that far exceed the logical limits of propriety, even for members of the peerage.*

INVEIGLE

in-VAY-guhl,
in-VEE-guhl

verb

To persuade or cajole with lies or flattery.

From French *aveugle* (blind or deluded), from Old French *avugle* (without eyes), from Medieval Latin *ab oculis* (away from the eyes).

Antonym: **DEHORT**

dee-HORT

verb

To deter, disadvise, or dissuade (someone).

From Latin *dehortari* (to dissuade) from *de-* (off, away) + *hortari* (to incite, to urge).

"And other there be that envegle mens daughters, in the contempt of their fathers, and go aboute to marry them wythout their consente."

—HUGH LATIMER,
2nd Sermon before
Kynges Maiestie, 1549

The honeyfuggling henchman used his cronyistic clout within the Knights of Pétomane to **inveigle** *his way into a position as an equerry or some such role at Mountebank Manor.*

EMPLEOMANIA

EM-plee-oh-MAY-nee-uh

noun

An excessive eagerness or zeal to hold public office.

From Spanish *empleomanía* (the desire for a government job), from *empleo* (job, employment), from Latin *implicare* (to engage, to involve), from *in-* (in) + *plicare* (to fold) + Ancient Greek -μανία (*manía*: madness).

Antonymous: **LAODICEAN**

LAY-oh-DISS-ee-uhn,
lay-OH-dih-SEE-uhn

noun

Someone apathetic or lackadaisical about politics or religion.

From Ancient Greek Λαοδίκεια (*Laodíkeia*, the name of several cities in Asia Minor), from Λαοδίκη (*Laodíkē*, a woman's name) + *-an*, from Old French *-ain*, from Latin *-anus* (adjectival suffix).

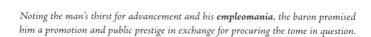

"The evil which has sapped the vigour of so many nations—'empleomania'— has made its insidious way into British administrative departments."

—GLASGOW HERALD, 1920

*Noting the man's thirst for advancement and his **empleomania**, the baron promised him a promotion and public prestige in exchange for procuring the tome in question.*

SNECK-DRAWING

SNEK-drah-ing

adjective

Crafty, cheating, or roguish.

From Scots *sneck* (latch), from Middle English *snekke*, from Old English *sneccan* + drawing (lifting, carrying), from Middle English *drawinge* (dragging, pulling, pushing), from Old English *dragende*.

Antonym: VERILOQUENT

Vehr-IHL-oh-kwehnt

adjective

Speaking truthfully or accurately, veracious.

From Latin *verus* (true, genuine) + *eloquens* (speaking, expressive), from *ex-* (out of) + *loqui* (to speak).

"Ye auld, snick-drawing dog!"

—Robert Burns,
*Poems, Chiefly in the
Scottish Dialect*, 1786

*Despite being a dimwitted dunderwhelp, the heinous henchman can play
the **sneck-drawing** snake when need arises.*

DEWDROPPER

DOO-drah-puhr,
DYOO-drah-puhr

noun

A person who revels all night and sleeps all day.

1920s flapper slang, perhaps from mountain dew (moonshine), from Middle English *dew*, from Old English *deaw* + dropper, from Middle English *droppe*, from Old English *dropa* (a drop) + -er, from Old English *-ere*, perhaps from Latin *-arius* (suffix of agency).

Antonymous: SOPHROSYNE

suh-FRAH-suh-nee

noun

Moderation, sound-mindedness, and good sense, especially in Ancient Greek art and philosophy.

From Ancient Greek σωφροσύνη (*sofrosúnē*: prudence, self-control), from σώφρων (*sófron*: moderate, sane), from σῶς (*sôs*: sound, whole) + φρήν (*frén*: mind, spirit) + -σύνη (*-súnē*: suffix of abstraction).

"'There's Liza, Tony's girlfriend. She's around somewhere, and Justin, our driver. He's a dewdropper.' Williams was not interested in finding out that a dewdropper was a man who stayed up all night. 'Are they still here?'"

—JAMES RUNCIE,
Sidney Chambers and the
Shadow of Death, 2012

*Some deviant **dewdropper** unwittingly acquired the coveted codex in a formidable footlocker full of bawdy facetiae won at auction of late.*

PICAROON

pih-kah-ROON

noun

An avaricious rogue always looking for easy money.

From Spanish *picarón* (feisty, naughty), from *pícaro* (rogue) + *-ón* (suffix of significance). Further origins unknown.

Antonym: **ELEEMOSYNARY**

EHL-uh-MAH-suh-NEHR-ee

noun

Someone who subsists on charity or who lives by receiving alms.

From Medieval Latin *eleemosynarius* (almsgiver), from Ancient Greek ἐλεημοσύνη (*eleēmosúnē*: alms), from ἔλεος (*éleos*: pity) + -μων (*-mon*: suffix of agency) + -σύνη (*-súnē*: suffix of abstraction) + Latin *-arius* (suffix of agency).

"Janet looked at him with the sly simplicity of her sect, and replied, 'Notwithstanding thy boasted honesty, friend, and although I am not accustomed to read and pass judgment on such volumes as thou hast submitted to my perusal, I think I see in thy countenance something of the pedlar— something of the picaroon.'"

—WALTER SCOTT, *Kenilworth*, 1821

The oblivious owner of the blightsome book has a rotten reputation as a profligate **picaroon***, so the suave soothsayer steels herself to spend surfeit specie to repurchase the purloined property.*

CHOUSE

(also: chowse)

CHAUSS

verb, noun

1. To trick, deceive, or cheat.

2. Someone who cheats, deceives, or tricks.

Perhaps from Ottoman Turkish جاوش (*çavuş*: messenger, sergeant); connection unclear.

Antonym: **TRUEPENNY**

TROO-peh-nee

noun

An honest fellow.

From Middle English *trewe*, from Old English *triewe* (faithful, trusty) + Middle English *peny*, from Old English *penig* (penny).

"He stole your Cloke, and pick'd your Pocket, Chews'd, and Caldes'd ye like a Block-head."

—SAMUEL BUTLER, *Hudibras*, 1664

*Paige Penwiper cheerfully chews over the chances of **chousing** the Vellwyn Vellum from its purse-proud plutocrat before he realizes that he possesses it.*

SLEEKIE

SLEE-kee

noun

A servile flatterer, a fawner.

From Scots *sleekit* (cunning, specious), from *sleek* (to deceive), from Old English *slic* (crafty, cunning, smooth).

Antonym: VITUPERATOR

vih-TOO-puhr-AY-tohr

noun

A person who censures abusively, a reprehender, a reviler.

From Latin *vitupero*, from *vitium* (defect, wrongdoing) + *parare* (to decide, to provide) + -tor (suffix of agency).

"The baggy, brosy, Baudrins braid,
Sae sleeky and sae slee."

—ROBERT BROWN, "Carlop Green," *Comic Poems of the Years 1685 and 1793*, 1817

*With the charisma to coax the quills off a porcupine, Winter Westhaven weaves a scheme that includes summoning the subterfuge of a sycophantic **sleekie**.*

ABYDOCOMIST

AH-bih-doh-COH-mist

noun

A sycophant or fawning flatterer who boasts of speaking falsely.

From Ancient Greek Ἀβυδοκόμης (*Abudokómēs*: Abydene), from Ἄβυδος (*Abudos* or Abydos in Egypt, its residents famous for boasting of their slanders), from Egyptian *ꜣbḏw* + Ancient Greek -κομείο (*-komeío*: locational suffix), from κομέειν (*koméein*: to care for) + -ιστής (*-istés*: suffix of agency).

Antonymous: **JANNOCK**

JAN-uhk

adjective

Honest, straightforward, fair, and generous.

Origin unknown. Perhaps related to genuine, from Latin *genuinus* (native, natural), from *gignere* (to bring forth), from Old Latin *genere* (to beget, to produce) + -ic, from Middle English *-ik*, from Old French *-ique*, from Latin *-icus* (adjectival suffix).

"The point of this expedition was to spend as much of Sand's gold as possible, only purchasing the most useless and cumbersome . . . including a massive rug from that abydocomist large enough to be its own small shop in this traveling market."

—M. Q. GELFAND, *Wraith*, 2017

*As the sneaky sleekie propounds the parlous plan, Oswin Otterbuck jibes at the malapert notion of honeyfuggling a common stranger like some kind of oleaginous **abydocomist**.*

PRINCOX

PRIN-koks, *PRING-koks*	**A coxcomb, a conceited person.**
noun	Origin unknown. Perhaps from prince, from Old French *prince* (leader, chief), from Latin *princeps* (first head), from *primus* (first) + *caput* (head) + cock (rooster) from Old English *cocc*, from Old French *coc*.

Antonymous: POCOCURANTE

POH-coh-koo- *RAHN-tay,* *POH-coh-kyoo-* *RAHN-tee*	**Characterized by lack of care, interest, or attention.**
adjective	From a character in *Candide* by Voltaire, from Italian *poco* (little), from Latin *paucus* + Italian *curante* (caring), from Latin *cura* (care) + *-ans* (participial suffix).

"Well-a-day—God save us from all such misproud princoxes!"

—Walter Scott, *Kenilworth,* 1821

*After arranging an introduction to the posh **princox** who possesses the grievous grimoire, the fashionable filcher selects the waterfront promenade for their rigged rendezvous.*

❊ SMELL-SMOCK ❊

SMEL-*smok*

noun

A person who chases women, a licentious man.

From Middle English *smellen*, from Old English *smyllan* (to smell, to emit fumes) + smock (woman's undergarment, a slip), from Middle English *smok*, from Old English *smocc* (an object slipped over or crept into).

Antonym: CAVALIER

KAV-uh-LEER

noun

A kind and courteous gentleman, particularly in regard to women.

From Middle French *cavalier* (horseman), from Old Italian *cavaliere* (knight, mounted soldier), from Old Occitan *cavalier*, from Latin *caballus* (horse), from Gaulish *caballos* (nag, old horse) + Latin *-arius* (suffix of agency).

"These attractions, and her petulant Deportment, drew on a number of Smell-smocks, which courted her for that Trifflle which men so much covet to enjoy and women to be rid of."

—RICHARD HEAD,
The Canting Academy, 1673

The fulsome fashionista prepares for all potentialities, including that the book's new owner has a reputation worse than that of the baron, a licentious **smell-smock.**

ECCEDENTESIAST

EK-ay-dehn-
TEE-zee-uhst

noun

An insincere person who fakes a smile.

From Latin *ecce* (behold, look here) + *dentes* (teeth) +
-*asta*, from Ancient Greek -αστής (-*astés*: verbal suffix).

Antonymous: **RIDIBUND**

RIH-dih-buhnd

adjective

Happy, lively, laughing easily.

From Latin *ridibundus*, from *ridere* (to laugh) + -*bundus*
(adjectival suffix).

"Put on your eccedentesiast mask!"

— KAREN DUFFY, *Backbone: Living with Chronic
Pain without Turning into One,* 2017

*A top-notch **eccedentesiast**, the beguiling bamboozler coquettishly cachinnates at the jocose
jobbernowl's juvenile jokes, while deftly demurring his distinctly distasteful advances.*

GOBEMOUCHE

GOHB-moosh noun	**A gullible person, someone who believes anything.** From French *gobemouche* (fly swallower), from *gober* (to gulp, to swallow whole), from Irish or Scots *gob* (beak, bill) + *mouche* (fly), from Old French *mousche*, from Latin *musca*.

PUHR-spih-KAY-shuh adjective	**Shrewdly discerning, keenly preceptive, gimlet-eyed.** From Latin *perspicax* (discerning, sharp-sighted), from *perspicere* (to look through, to perceive), from *per-* (through) + *specere* (to behold, to observe) + *-ax* (suffix of inclination) + *-osus* (adjectival suffix).

"Those Continental gobemouches whose gift for believing the incredible almost approaches to genius."

—PALL MALL GAZETTE, 1884

At the end of the esplanade, the honeyfuggling heister convinces the goatish **gobemouche** *that they should go back to his place to admire his "art collection."*

STAGMIRE

STAG-my-uhr

noun

1. A predicament, a difficult situation.

2. An awkward, ill-gaited person.

Regional: Yorkshire. Origin unknown. Perhaps from stag, from Middle English *stagge*, from Old English *stagga* + mire (deep mud, a predicament), from Middle English *mire*, from Old Norse *mýrr*.

Antonymous: LEGGIADROUS

leh-gee-ADD-ruhs

adjective

Graceful, elegant, pleasing.

From Italian *leggiadro*, from *leggiadria* (elegance, loveliness), from Old Occitan *leujairia*, from Medieval Latin *leviarius*, from Latin *levis* (light, not heavy) + *-arius* (suffix of agency) + *-osus* (adjectival suffix).

"The army . . . retired, uncunningly to a part called The Stagmire, where there was no passage."

—ROBERT LINDSAY,
The Historie and Cronicles of Scotland, 1728

*A splenetic **stagmire**, the henchman lumbers from the shrubbery and hoiks the heister's would-be roué over his shoulder, like a stevedore hauling a bag of potatoes.*

GONGOOZLER

gahn-GOOZ-luhr,
gahng-GOOZ-luhr

noun

Someone who sits and stares for prolonged periods.

Regional: Lincolnshire. Perhaps from gawn + gooze (both: to gape, to stare) + -er, from Old English -ere, perhaps from Latin -arius (suffix of agency).

Antonymous: **SPIZZERINCTUM**

spih-zuhr-INK-tuhm

noun

The passion and drive to succeed.

Regional: America, from spizarinctum (cash, money), perhaps from specie, from Latin *specie*, from *specere* (to observe, to watch) + -ies (suffix of abstraction) + -ing, from Old English -ing (verbal suffix) + Latin -tum (suffix of abstraction).

"Please tell me why you British will not commit yourselves wholeheartedly to the Single European Currency and the European Community, asked the gongoozler. You are not being reasonable and I wish you to explain."

—TERRY DARLINGTON,
Narrow Dog to Carcassonne, 2008

During the kerfuffle, the wheedling wangler lands, tuchus over teakettle,
on the ground like a woolgathering **gongoozler***, unsure what just transpired.*

SLUTHERMUCK

SLUH-*thuhr-muhk*

noun

An idle, dirty person.

Regional: Yorkshire. From sluther (to slide, to slither), from slither, from Middle English *slitheren*, from Old English *slidrian* + muck, from Middle English *muk*, from Old Norse *myki* (dung) or perhaps Old English *moc* (pig dung).

Antonymous: **PREEKIT**

PREE-*kiht*

adjective

1. Smartly dressed, dapper.

2. Foppish, dandified.

Regional: Scotland, from Scots *prick* (to fasten with a pin), from Old Scots *prik* (a knitting needle), from Old English *priccan* (to prick).

"Bed-huntin' starts abaht nah. Sally Sluthermuck lets it start abaht t' thirty't' o' Auagust, an' then a-stead o' shoo huntin' t' fleeas, t' fleeas hunt her."

— from *Tommy Toddles's Comic Almenac*, 1865

The leesome librarian and benefic bibliopole help the fetching fabulist find their feet as they sling slurs at the slovenly **sluthermuck** *who preemptively put paid to the party's plan.*

DOWFART

DAU-fahrt,
DOH-fahrt

noun

1. A dull, foolish, or stupid person.

2. Someone without courage or destitute of spirit.

3. Melancholy.

Regional: Scotland. From Scots *dowf* (dull, melancholy, slow), from Old Scots *dolf* (dull, heavy, spiritless), from Old Norse *daufr* (deaf), perhaps influenced by doaf, variant of doof + -art (suffix of agency), from Middle English *-ard*, from Old French *-ard*.

Antonymous: **SÇAVOIR**

sav-WAHR

noun

Sharpness, cunning.

From Middle French *sçavoir* (to know), from Old French *savoir*, from Latin *sapere* (to taste) + *scire* (to know).

"Wha could refuse the lassie's fair demand? A dowfart might."

—RICHARD GALL,
Poems & Songs, 1819

The proficuous polyhistor scoffingly recognizes the brigandish baron's dullard
dowfart *of a henchman, who bodily purloined their mark in plain view.*

MALVERSATION

MAL-*vuhr*-SAY-*shun*

noun

Evil conduct, fraudulent action, or misbehavior at work by means of extortion, fraud, or breach of trust.

From French *malversation*, from Middle French *malverser*, from Latin *male versari* (to behave badly), from *malus* (bad, evil) + *versere* (to move around, to think over), from *vertere* (to turn, to reverse) + *-atio*, variant of *-tio* (nominative suffix).

Antonymous: **SEVENDLE**

suh-VEHN-*duhl*

adjective

1. Trustworthy, dependable.

2. Strong, secure, firm.

Regional: Scotland. From Scots *solvendie* (of people: strong, healthy), from Latin *solvendo*, from *solvere* (to release, to relax), from *se-* (away) + *luere* (to cleanse, to purge).

"Those malversations in office; those neglects of duty; the disobedience of orders; . . . more certainly than the plots of all the French partisans, are passed unnoticed."

—Arthur Wellesley, Viscount Wellington, "To Colonel Gordon, Commissary in Chief," 12th June 1811

No doubt the brazen baron, whose rapacious reach knows no bounds, goaded his galumphing glorified gofer into performing such a malevolent act of **malversation.**

JACKANAPES

JAK-uh-NAYPZ noun	**1. An impudent or conceited person.**
	2. A saucy or mischievous child.
	3. A monkey.
	From "Jack of Naples," referring specifically to William de la Pole, 1st Duke of Suffolk, whose coat of arms featured an ape's clog (a weight and chain used to restrain monkeys, which Naples exported to England at the time) or generally to a monkey, from Jack (generic name for a man of low social standing), from Middle English *Jankin*, from John + -kin (diminutive suffix), from Middle English *-kin*, perhaps from Middle Dutch *-ken* + of, from Old English *af* (from) + Naples, from Latin *Neapolis*, from Ancient Greek Νεάπολις (Neápolis), from νέα (néa: new) + πόλις (pólis: city).

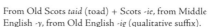

Antonym: **TAIDIE**

TEH-dee noun	**A much-loved child, a child regarded with tenderness.**
	From Old Scots *taid* (toad) + Scots *-ie*, from Middle English *-y*, from Old English *-ig* (qualitative suffix).

"Now, Jackanapes, I think you're fitted
For all the stuff with which you twitted
Those whom you ought t'adore, at least
To own superior, for if ceased."

—THE LONDON CHRONICLE or the
UNIVERSAL EVENING POST, 1760

The cowering captive conceded the cache of concupiscent coloring books, then shoved a shipload of shillings at the gigantic **jackanapes** *to curtail the calamitous confrontation.*

CUSTRIL

(also: custrel, coistrel, cuistrel)

KUSS-truhl

noun

A fool, dolt, or silly person.

From Middle English *custrell* (a knight's squire), from Old French *coustillier* (a kind of soldier), from *coustille* (double-edged sword) + *-ier* (suffix of profession), from Latin *-arius* (suffix of agency).

Antonymous: **THOUGHTISH**

THAHK-tish

adjective

Gravely thoughtful, serious.

From Scots *thocht*, (thought) from Old Scots *thoght*, from Old English *thoht* + *-ish*, from Old English *-isc* (suffix of similarity).

"I'll drink to her as long as there is a passage in my throat and drink in Illyria: he's a coward and a coystrill that will not drink to my niece till his brains turn o' the toe like a parish-top."

—William Shakespeare, *Twelfth Night*, 1623

*The hagriding henchman proffers his patron the vile volume heretofore held by the craven **custril**, whom he diabolically dragooned by defenestration.*

GASCONADE

gas-kuhn-AYD

verb

To bluster, boast, brag, or vaunt.

From French *gasconnade*, from *Gascon* (someone from Gascony), from Middle French *Gascon*, from Latin *Vascones* (a pre-Roman tribe of the Basque people) + French *-ade*, from Latin *-atus* (suffix of appearance).

Antonymous: **PUDENCY**

PYOO-dehn-see

noun

Modesty, reserve, shamefacedness.

From Latin *pudentia*, from *pudere* (to be ashamed, to shame).

"'Did it save your coat?' says Talleyrand. 'I hear they tore it when they threw you out. Don't gasconade to me. You may be in the road of victory, but you aren't there yet.'"

—RUDYARD KIPLING,
Rewards and Fairies, 1899

*The bumptious baron tires of his halfwitted henchman's gloaty **gasconading** and demands to see the object of his nefarious desires tout de suite.*

FANFARONADE

FAN-fahr-uh-NAYD

noun

Swaggering ostentation, vain boasting or bluster.

From French *fanfaronnade* (swagger, boastful), from Spanish *fanfarrón*, from Arabic فَرْفَار (farfār).

Antonym: DULCILOQUY

duhl-SILL-oh-kwee

noun

A soft manner of speaking, a whisper.

From Latin *dulcis* (sweet) + *loqui* (to speak).

"He damned her ingratitude; She, his fanfarronade."

—Robert Bage, *Barham Downs*, 1784

*After years of searching for the elusive Vellwyn Vellum, the bombastic baron vociferates his victory with flamboyant **fanfaronade**.*

PLUNDERBUND

PLUHN-duhr-buhnd

noun

A political or financial cabal engaged in exploiting the public; a thieving group of businessmen.

Regional: America. From plunder, from German *plündern* (to loot), from Middle Low German *plunderen* + bund, from German *bund* (alliance, league), from Middle High German *binden*, from Old High German *bintan*.

Antonym: MAECENAS

mye-SEE-nuhs

noun

A munificent benefactor or generously charitable patron, particularly of the arts.

From Latin *maecenas* (literary patron), from Gaius Cilnius Maecenas, patron of Roman poets Horace and Virgil.

"The trust against which the people complain is . . . the thieving trust—the trust which belongs to the Plunderbund."

—*NEWARK ADVOCATE* (Ohio), 1902

Not satisfied with merely belonging to the secret ranks of a **plunderbund**, *the backhanded baron seeks to bend the world itself to his demented desiderata.*

COLLYBIST

KAH-lih-bist

noun

A usurer or miser.

From Latin *collybista* (banker, money changer), from Ancient Greek κόλλυβος (*kóllubos*: small coin) + -ιστής (*-istés*: suffix of agency).

Antonymous: FLAHOOLICK

flah-HOOL-ohk

adjective

Generous and giving in a showy way, munificent; characteristic of a big spender.

From Irish *flaithiúlach* (generous), from *flaithiúil* (munificent, lavish), from Old Irish *flaithemail* (princely, munificent), perhaps from *flaith* (lordship, sovereignty) + *-úil* (suffix of similarity) + *-ach* (adjectival suffix).

"For, certes, no man of a low degree
May bid two guestes, or gout, or usurie:
Unlesse some base hedge-creeping Collybist
Scatters his refuse scraps on whom he list,
For Easter-gloves, or for a Shroftide hen,
Which, bought to give, he takes to sell agen."

—JOSEPH HALL, "Satire V,"
Virgidemiarum, 1598

Lord Greensquire harbors a seething animosity for his rival and superior, the marquess of Mitherton, a closehanded **collybist** *clutching the strings of political power.*

GREASEHORN

GREES-hohrn

noun

1. A horn filled with grease for lubricating purposes.

2. A toadyish, sycophantic person; a brown-nosing flatterer; someone obsequiously attached to another.

Regional: Yorkshire. From grease, from Middle English *grece*, from Old French *graisse*, from Latin *crassus* (fat, thick), from Old Latin *cartsus* + horn, from Old English *horn*.

Antonym: **AUTOCEPHALON**

ah-toh-SEHF-uh-lahn

noun

An independent thinker, someone who thinks and behaves according to a moral code.

From Ancient Greek αὐτοκέφαλος (*autoképhalos*: independent, autonomous), from αὐτός (*autos*: self) + κεφαλή (*kephalé*: head).

"Smooth-faced, snivelling greasehorn!"

— CHARLOTTE BRONTË, *The Professor*, 1857

The blandishing baron has been playing the **greasehorn** *to the megalomaniacal marquess, obsequiously currying favor while meticulously machinating his supplantation.*

SNOLLYGOSTER

SNAH-lee-GAH-stuhr

noun

A shrewd person unguided by principles, particularly a politician.

Regional: America. Perhaps from snallygaster (a beast that preys on chickens and children), perhaps from Pennsylvania German *schnelle geeschter*, from German *schnell* (quick), from Old High German *snel* (brave, quick) + German *geister* (spirits), from Old High German *geist* (ghost).

Antonym: BAWCOCK

BAH-kahk,
BOH-kahk

noun

A fine fellow.

From Old French *baud* (bold, brave) + cock (rooster) from Old English *cocc*, from Old French *coc*.

"A Georgia editor kindly explains that 'a snollygoster is a fellow who wants office, regardless of party, platform or principles, and who, whenever he wins, gets there by the sheer force of monumental talknophical assumnacy."

— *Columbus Dispatch* (Ohio), 1895

*The marquess of Mitherton considers Baron Greensquire a snidely **snollygoster**, believing that he can dispatch him whenever and however he likes.*

PLEBICOLIST

pleh-BIK-uh-list

noun

Someone who courts the favor of the common people, a populist, a demagogue.

From Latin *plebicola*, from *plebs* (the people) + *colere* (to cultivate) + *-ista*, from Ancient Greek -ιστής (*-istés:* suffix of agency).

Antonym: WHEEDLER

WEED-luhr

noun

A person who entices with cajoling, coaxing, flattery, or soft words.

Origin unknown, perhaps from Middle English *wedlen* (to beg), from Old English *wædlian* (to be poor, to beg) or perhaps from German *wedeln* (to wag one's tail), from Middle High German *wedelen*, variant of *wadelen* (to wander, to waver), from Old High German *wadalon* (to rove, to wander) + *-er*, from Old English *-ere*, perhaps from Latin *-arius* (suffix of agency).

"Alva Adams, the plausible plebicolist who for so many had prostituted Colorado to the lust of lucre and enslaved her to the corporations to serve his personal ends, was in his political death-struggle and fighting with the desperation of a dog-doomed rat."

—WALTER HURT,
The Scarlet Shadow, 1907

*The bourgeois baron has been honing his skills as a **plebicolist** while simultaneously playing the role of adulatory apple-polisher to the mighty marquess.*

QUOCKERWODGER

KWAH-kuhr-
WAH-juhr

noun

1. A wooden toy that jerks its limbs when pulled by a string.

2. A puppet politician, an official controlled by someone else.

British slang, mid-1800s, origin unknown.

Antonymous: **METTLESOME**

MEHT-uhl-suhm

adjective

Full of mettle or spirit, courageous, fiery.

From mettle, variant of metal, from Old French *metal*, from Latin *metallum* (mine, metal quarry) from Ancient Greek μέταλλον (*métallon*).

"The shameless arts of the sycophant are not monopolised by Mr. Quocker-wodger and his congeners."

—WILLIAM NATION,
"A Tongue in a Tree,"
Satires: Political and Social,
volume 2, 1880

The marquess thinks that he's made a **quockerwodger** *of the baron, but the latter has been playing a game of Grimalkin and Murine, precisely positioning the dominoes of doom.*

PANJANDRUM

pan-JAN-druhm

noun

An arrogant, boorish, pompous person in a position of authority.

....

A nonce word coined by dramatist Samuel Foote to test the memory of actor Charles Macklin, who claimed the ability to repeat any text perfectly after hearing it only once.

Antonym: VOTARIST

VO-tuh-rist

noun

1. Someone consecrated, devoted, or engaged by a vow or promise.

....

2. A person passionate about a particular service, study, or state of life.

....

From votary, from Latin *votus*, from *vovere* (to devote, to vow) + *-arius* (suffix of agency) + *-ista*, from Ancient Greek -ιστής (*-istés*: suffix of agency).

"There were abbots and prelates, knights and squires, and all who delighted to honor the great panjandrum of Rheims."

—EBENEZER COBHAM BREWER, *Character Sketches of Romance, Fiction and the Drama,* 1892

---

*With baleful laughter, the perfidious **panjandrum** holds aloft his plundered prize, the key to world domination, then settles down to extract its powerful secrets.*

FLAPDOODLE

FLAP-doo-duhl

noun

1. Food for fools.

2. Transparent pretense or nonsense, such as gross flattery, nonsensical talk, or foolish boasting.

Regional: America. Origin unknown, perhaps from flap, from Middle English *flap* (a blow or something flexible or loose) + doodle, from Low German *dudeltopf* (simpleton), from *dudeln* (to play monotone or simple music).

Antonymous: VERIDICAL

vuh-RIH-dih-kuhl

adjective

Honest, truthful, veracious.

From Latin *veridicus* (truthfully spoken), from *verus* (true) + *dicere* (to say) + *-alis* (adjectival suffix).

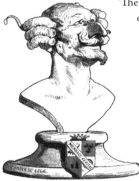

"The gentleman has eaten no small quantity of flapdoodle in his lifetime. . . . It's the stuff they feed fools on."

—FREDERICK MARRYAT,
Peter Simple, 1834

A beleaguered look overtakes the baron's face as he peruses the pages of the pandect, which resemble a load of fanciful **flapdoodle** *and frivolous folderol.*

❧ BEDLAMITE ❧

BED-luh-meit

noun

A lunatic or maniac.

From bedlam, reduced from Bethlehem, reduced from St. Mary of Bethlehem Hospital (a London asylum for the insane) + -ite, from French -*ite*, from Latin -*ites*, from Ancient Greek -ίτης (-*ítēs*: suffix of association).

Antonymous: **SAPIENT**

SAY-pee-uhnt

adjective

Sagacious, wise.

From Old French *sapient*, from Latin *sapiens* (judicious, wise), from *sapere* (to know, to understand).

"But when they reach'd their own apartments, there,
  Like birds, or boys, or bedlamites broke loose . . .
  Their guards being gone, and as it were a truce
  Establish'd between them and bondage, they
  Began to sing, dance, chatter, smile, and play."

— GEORGE GORDON, LORD BYRON,
  from Canto VI, *Don Juan*, 1823

*Loudly lamenting, the bedaffled baron believes that a barmy **bedlamite**, some arreptitious architect of bushwa blatherings and cockamamie claptrap, elucubrated this book.*

RAWGABBIT

RAH-gab-iht

noun

Someone who speaks confidently on topics beyond one's knowledge.

Regional: Scotland. From Middle English *raw*, from Old English *hreaw* (uncooked) + Scots *gabbit* (morsel, mouthful), from *gobbet* (a lump, piece), from Middle French *gobet*, from *gober* (to gulp, to swallow whole), from Irish or Scots *gob* (beak, bill).

Antonymous: **RUMGUMPTION**

ruhm-GUHMP-shuhn

noun

1. Rough or basic common sense.

2. Keenness of intellect, understanding.

From Scots *ram-* (prefix of intensification), from English slang rum (excellent, fine, great), perhaps from Romani *rom* (husband, man) + Scots *gumption* (common sense, shrewdness), perhaps from Middle English *gome*, from Old Norse *gaumr* (attention, heed) + Latin *-tio* (nominative suffix).

"Now they all come out: the rumours, furphies, and strange tidings—the pure joy of being a rawgabbit and a spermologer."

—MARK FORSYTH,
The Horologicon, 2012

Sighing sciolistically, the riled **rawgabbit** *vaingloriously commits himself to comprehending the cacography contained within the pages of the musty tome.*

VLOTHER

VLAH-thuhr
noun

Babblement, balderdash, bushwa, nonsense.

Regional: Somerset. Origin unknown, perhaps a variant of blather, from Middle English *bloderen*, from Old Norse *blaðra* (to talk nonsense).

Antonym: EPEXEGESIS

eh-PEHK-suh-JEE-sis
noun

The providing of additional words to clarify meaning.

From Ancient Greek ἐπεξήγησις (epexégēsis), from ἐπί (*epí-*: in addition to, around) + ἐξηγέεσθαι (*exēgésthai*: to describe, to explain), from ἐκ- (*ek-*: away) + ἡγέεσθαι (hēgéesthai: to lead, to precede).

"At all tha fayers an revels too
Tom Gook war shower ta be,
A takin vlother vast awa,—
A hoopin who bit he."

—from "Tom Gool, and Luck in tha Bag," *The Dialect of the West of England; Particularly Somersetshire*, compiled by James Jennings, 1825/1869

*Lord Greensquire intones the vacuitous **vlother** inscribed upon the parchment, its arcana echoing off the walls of his capacious family crypt.*

IV

CORPOREAL
CATASTROPHES

(BODILY BUMMERS)

CROOCHIE-PROOCHLES

KROO-chee-
PROO-chuhls

plural noun

The fidgety feeling of sitting in a cramped position or crowded environment.

From Scots *crooky*, from Middle English *crok*, from Old English *crōc* (bend, hook) + Middle English *-y*, from Old English *-ig* (qualitative suffix) + prickles, from Middle English *prikle*, from Old English *pricle*, from *priccan* (to prick) + *-lian* (suffix of frequency).

"A friend describes the sensation of return to the office stool after holiday in the open thus: 'I am suffering from an attack of croochie-proochles, and it will be some time before I get over it.'"

— oral source, SCOTTISH NATIONAL DICTIONARY, 1923

*Stultifying silence fills the undercroft as **croochie-proochles** begin tormenting Sebastian Mountebank, 4th Baron Greensquire.*

FURFURACEOUS

fuhr-fuhr-AY-shuss

adjective

1. Flaky.

....

2. Covered in or afflicted with dandruff.

....

From Latin *furfur* (chaff, grain husks, a skin infection) + -aceous (suffix of a certain kind), from Latin *-ax* (suffix of inclination) + *-eus* (suffix of origin).

"The upper Chap of the Bill is half cover'd . . . with a naked, white, tuberous, furfuraceous Flesh."

—JOHN MOORE, *Columbarium: Or, the Pigeon-house*, 1735

*In his mounting mania, the barmy baron believes that he can hear the **furfuraceous** fungus whisper from the moldering walls of the frowzy sepulcher.*

HURPLE

(also: hurkle)	**To contract and raise the back or**
HUHR-puhl	**shoulders from a sensation of cold.**
verb	

Regional: Yorkshire. From Scots *hurkle* (to crouch for secrecy or warmth, to shrug the shoulders), from Old Scots *hurkill*, from Middle English *hurkle*, from *hurk* (to crouch by a fire, to root in dirt) + -le, from Middle English -*len*, from Old English -*lian* (suffix of frequency).

"Another sadly fixing his eies on the ground, and hurckling with his head to his sholders, foohishly imagind, that Atlas being faint, & weary of his burthen, would shortly let the heavens fall upon his head, and break his crag."

—THOMAS WALKINGTON, *The Optick Glasse of Humors*, 1607

*On tenterhooks, the avaricious aristocrat **hurples** with a shiversome shudder as the air in the vaulted chamber becomes bewilderingly brumal.*

PLOOK

PLEWK

noun

A pimple.

Regional: Yorkshire. From Scots *plouk* (pustule, protuberance), from Old Scots *plukkit* (pimpled), perhaps from Middle Low German *pluck* (a plug, a bung).

"Jock's luckless feature was his nose . . . Wi'
plooks set roond like curran' berries."

—*Arbroath Guide,* 1892

In the misty darkness, something reminiscent of a gigantic, suppurating
plook *emerges, as if squeezed through some unseen aperture.*

WAMBLE

WAHM-buhl

verb

1. **To weave unsteadily, to stagger.**

2. **To writhe or shake.**

3. **To rumble and heave, to suffer from nausea.**

From Middle English *wamlen*, from Latin *vomere* (to vomit, to emit) + -le, from Middle English *-len*, from Old English *-lian* (suffix of frequency).

"Our meat going downe into the stomacke merily, and with pleasure, dissolveth incontinently all wambles."

—PHILEMON HOLLAND, *Plutarch's Morals*, 1603

*Growing and distorting, the gibbous pustule plops to the floor with a disquieting squelch and wobblingly **wambles** around, as though suffering from naupathia.*

BORBORYGMUS

bor-buhr-IG-muhs

noun

The rumbling noise caused by wind in the intestines.

From Ancient Greek βορβορυγμός (*borborugmós*: a fart), from βορβορύζειν (*borborúzein*: to rumble) + -μός (*-mós*: suffix of abstraction).

"Borborygmi . . . are a serious annoyance, and on occasions a misfortune, as, for instance, when they trouble the sufferer in a select company during a pause in general conversation."

—L i o n e l B e a l e , *On Slight Ailments*, 1 8 8 0

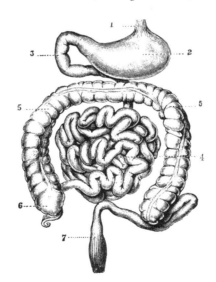

Borborygmus *reverberates through the crypt while the abomination, resembling aspic left in the summer sun, swells like a surfaced blobfish.*

PERHORRESCE

puhr-hohr-ESS

verb

To tremble, shudder, or quake in terror.

From Latin *perhorrescere* (to shudder intensely), from *per-* (thoroughly) + *horrescere* (to dread, to tremble), from *horrere* (to tremble) + *-scere* (suffix of beginning).

"Scarcely a decade ago most of us would have perhorresced the idea that there could be a seven years' course of Bible study adopted in common by most of the Protestant sects."

—*PRINCETON REVIEW*, 1882

*Twiglike appendages punch through the sizeable circumference of the ghastly gobbet, prompting the bilious baron to **perhorresce** and swoon.*

SUPPURATION

SUHP-uhr-AY-shun,
SUHP-yuhr-AY-shun

noun

1. The formation of pus.

2. Pus itself, as from an infected wound.

From Latin *suppuratio* (abscess, festering under
the surface), from *sub-* (below) + *pus* (pus) + *-tio*
(nominative suffix).

"The force of the blood acting continually against the sides
of the artery . . . wastes away that part of the cyst, gives
rise to obstructions and suppurations of the bone."

—PHILOSOPHICAL SOCIETY OF EDINBURGH,
Essays and Observations, 1771

The prodigious plook, now the size of a potbellied pig, explodes like a putrid
profiterole, splattering the charnel chamber with sloppy **suppuration.**

COLLYWOBBLES

KAH-lee-WAH-buhlz
plural noun

Discomfort or illness related to cramping in or looseness of the bowels.

Perhaps from colic (gastrointestinal pain), from French *colique*, from Latin *colica*, from Ancient Greek κωλικός (*kolikós*: colonic suffering), from κῶλον (*kôlon*: body part) + -ικός (*-ikós*: adjectival suffix) + wobble, variant of wabble, perhaps from Low German *wabbeln* (to wobble).

"After a time, however, he gives way to the indulgence, having received the solemn assurances of his companions that it is absolutely necessary to preserve his health, and keep him from getting the collywobbles in his pandenoodles."

—"JOSEPH MUFF,"
"The Physiology of the London Medical Student," *Punch*, 1841

*The bespattered baron realizes that reflexive retching and colitic **collywobbles** disagree in both principle and action.*

ENCOPRESIS

ehn-kuh-PREE-sis

noun

The disagreeable condition of having frequent, involuntary fecal events, a shitstorm.

From Latin *encopresis*, from Ancient Greek ἐγκόπρησις (*enkóprēsis*), from ἐν- (*en-*: in) + κόπρος (*kópros*: excrement) + -ητικός (*-ētikós*: adjectival suffix).

"To receive a diagnosis of encopresis, the child must pass feces into inappropriate places (such as clothing or on the floor) at least once per month for three months or more."

—CHRISTINA LOW KAPALU AND
EDWARD CHRISTOPHERSEN,
"Fact Sheet: Encopresis in Children and Adolescents,"
PedPsych.org, 2019

*Few needs in life rally cathexis like the want of a commode, and the dead, unmoved with such corporeal concerns as **encopresis**, lack such an item in their place of rest.*

IMBULBITATE

ihm-BUHL-bih-tayt
verb

To defecate oneself.

From Latin *in-* (in) + *bulbus* (edible bulb), from Ancient Greek βολβός (*bolbós*: root vegetable) + βόλιτον (*bóliton*: cow dung) + Latin *-atus* (suffix of appearance).

"Be grateful for small favors—at least you weren't inflicted with imbulbitation."

—NANCY COLLINS, *Right Hand Magic*, 2010

From the ooze, hideous creatures skitter toward Lord Greensquire as he **imbulbitates**, *bemiring his britches and crying, "They're going to devour me!"—and so they do.*

INFANDOUS

ihn-FAN-duhs

adjective

Too horrific or monstrous for words.

From Latin *infandus* (unspeakable, abominable) from *in-* (without, not) + *fandus* (something to be spoken), from *fari* (to say, to talk).

"Nor would it be an unwise part, if amongst other Learned Professors at the University of Leyden, or elsewhere, there were a meet maintainance order'd for a Professor of Astronomy, mixed with Astrology, if any should fancy such an Union of Science, to give some, it may be, more than probable warning of such Infandous Cataclysmes, Pictures, and Assurances of Noah's Floud, that at least the life of Thousands may be saved."

—John Goad, *Astro-meteorologica*, 1686

*The ethereal warble emanating from the gaping aperture gradually drowns out the ghastly **infandous** murmuring of monomaniacal mastication.*

SIDERATION

sih-duhr-AY-shuhn

noun

1. A sudden, inexplicable illness or event caused by heavenly bodies.

2. The state of being starstruck.

From Latin *sideratio*, from *sidus* (star, constellation), perhaps related to Ancient Greek σίδηρος (*sídēros*: iron, meteorite) + Latin *-tio* (nominative suffix).

"Rabid animals, which, by a most unaccountable syderation
from Heaven, had now neither strength nor sense left
'em to do anything for their own defence."

—JAMES MURRAY,
A New English Dictionary on Historical Principles, 1919

The door to the crypt crashes open to reveal the heroic quintet, whose dramatic derring-do immediately melts into **sideration** *upon seeing the unspeakable horrors within.*

⋆⟨ FEIST ⟩⋆

FYST

noun

Clandestine, inaudible flatulence; a tacit but toxic fart.

From Middle English *fyste* (to break wind), from Old English *fystung* (stinking).

"But she was a foule slut,
For her mouth fomyd
And her bely groned:
Jone sayne she had eaten a fyest.
'By Christ,' sayde she, 'thou lyest.
I have as swete a breth
As thou, wyth shamful deth!'"

—John Skelton, *The Tunnying of Elynour Rummyng,* 1529

*Oswin Otterbuck releases a spicy little **feist** as the group, beholding what little remains of the baron's body, ponders the ineffable ghastliness before them.*

WOOFITS

WOO-fitz

plural noun

1. A moody depression.

....

2. An unwell feeling, especially a headache.

....

3. A hangover.

....

Origin unknown, perhaps from woe, from Middle English *wo*, from Old English *wā* + fit (frenzy), perhaps from Old English *fitt* (conflict).

"Curtis says he is suffering from the Woofits, that dread disease that comes from overeating and underdrinking."

—JOHN McGAVOCK GRIDER,
War Birds: Diary of an Unknown Aviator, 1926

Waylaid by woeful **woofits,** *Winter Westhaven slues across the threshold, clearing a path that enables the others to enter and perform the dwimmer of banishment.*

CRAPULOUS

KRAP-yoo-luhs
adjective

Unwell as a result of intemperance, especially overindulgence in alcohol.

From Latin *crapulosus* (drunk), from *crapula* (intoxication), from Ancient Greek κραιπάλη (*kraipálē*: intoxication, hangover) + Latin -*osus* (adjectival suffix).

"I find no impeachment of his morals deserving of attention—
and he certainly must have been a man of very great temperance,
for the business and studies through which he went would be
enough to fill up the lives of ten men who spend their evenings
over their wine, and awake crapulous in the morning."

—John Campbell, "Life of Lord [Francis] Bacon,"
The Lives of the Lord Chancellors, 1845

*Feeling curiously **crapulous**, the apotropaic entourage gathers within the mirificent manor to recuperate from the pernicious pains of the baleful brume.*

NIDOROSITY

nih-duhr-AH-sih-tee

noun

Eructation that tastes of undigested meat, a beefy burp.

From Latin *nidorosus* (smelling like cooked animal), from *nidor* (the smell or steam from cooking animals) + *-osus* (adjectival suffix) + *-ity*, from Old French *-ite*, from Latin *-itas* (nominative suffix).

"The Cure of this Nidorosity, is, 1. By Evacuation, by Vomiting and Purging, as is directed."

—JOHN FLOYER, *The Preternatural State of Animal Humours*, 1696

Nuisanced by noisome **nidorosity,** *the queasy conservator ruminates that the pandemonium in the crypt could have proven far worse.*

FUMOSITIES

foo-MAH-sih-teez

plural noun

Foul fumes detected on belched breath.

From Middle English *fumosite*, from Old French *fumosité*, from Latin *fumositas*, from *fumus* (fume, smoke) + *-osus* (adjectival suffix) + *-itas* (nominative suffix).

"Belche thou neare to no mans face with a corrupt fumosytye, but turne from such occasyon, friend, hate such ventositye."

—HUGH RHODES, *The Boke of Nurture*, 1530

The lad's **fumosities** *could blow a buzzard off a buffalo carcass, which encourages Paige Penwiper to put distance between herself and his bilious burping.*

135

BDOLOTIC

duh-LAH-tik

adjective

Inclined to farting.

From Ancient Greek βδέειν (*bdéein*: to fart) + -λ- (-*l*-: interfix) + -ωτικός (-*otikós*: adjectival suffix).

"To the horror of her hapless niece, old Mrs. Grubowski not only grew more and more violently drunk as the evening progressed, but increasingly bdolotic, as well."

—PETER NOVOBATZKY AND AMMON SHEA, *Depraved English*, 1999

Evading the effluvia, Verbena Vellwyn ponders how the **bdolotic** *dowfart's inability to articulate arcane allophones averted assured annihilation.*

NAUPATHIA

nah-PATH-ee-uh,
now-PATH-ee-uh

noun

Motion sickness related to water,
mal de mer, seasickness.

From Ancient Greek ναῦς (*naûs*: ship) + πάθος (*páthos*: suffering) + -ία (*-ía*: suffix of abstraction).

"The most generally accepted theory of the causation (*Med. Abstract*) of sea-sickness is that which attributes it to an influence on the circulation of the cerebral cortex produced by the oscillation of the ship, thus accounting for the gastric symptoms. This will not, however, explain all cases of naupathia."

—from "New Theory of Sea-Sickness,"
Medical Argus, volume 6, number 8, 1896

Beholding the conservator's esophageal struggle, the fashionmonger feels woozily worsted with a sensation not entirely dissimilar to **naupathia**.

SNORK

(also: snurk)	**To snore, snort, or snuffle.**
SNOHRK	
verb	Regional: Scotland. From Scots *snork* (to snore), from Middle Low German *snorken* (to snore, to snort).

"The old grouting wretch kept up such a snorking and yellyhooing."

—SAMUEL CROCKETT, *The Grey Man*, 1896

*The muculent modiste loudly **snorks** into a kerchief, startling a flumpet-like flatus from the auguring heiress, which sends the conjuring conservator into great gales of laughter.*

SNURT

SNUHRT

verb

To eject mucus from the nose, as when sneezing.

From Scots *snurt*, variant of snot, influenced by snort, from Middle English *snorten*, from *snoren*, from Old English *fnora*.

"Give him liberty to hold downe his head,
and to snurt out the filthy matter."

—GERVASE MARKHAM, *Maister-Peece*, 1610

*The thouchtish thaumaturge warns the feverish fashionista, who continues snorking into their kerchief, not to strain their friendship by **snurting** on her person.*

139

RHINORRHEA

RYE-nuh-REE-uh

noun

**Excessive secretion of mucus
from the nose.**

From Ancient Greek ῥινο- (*rhino-*: nasal), from ῥίς (*rhís*: nose) + -ῥοία (*-rhoía*: flowing), from ῥέειν (*rhéein*: to flow) + -ία (*-ía*: suffix of abstraction).

"The affection known by the name of Ozæna, or Rhinorrhœa, often the source of the greatest misery and suffering, the author divides into three varieties—the catarrhal, scrofulous, and syphilitic."

—*The Lancet,* 1856

*Offering the snorking swank an unsullied mouchoir for their refractory **rhinorrhea**, the liverish librarian recommends a diverting game of Veritas or Venture.*

FORSWUNK

(also: forswunke)

fohr-SWUHNK

adjective

Extremely exhausted after physical exertion.

From Middle English *forswunken*, from *forswinken* (to overwork), from Old English *for-* (completely) + Middle English *swinken*, from Old English *swincan* (to labor, to struggle).

"Soone as my younglings cryen for the dam,
To her will I offer a milkwhite Lamb:
Shee is my goddesse plaine,
And I her shepherds swayne,
Albee forswonck and forswatt I am."

—EDMUND SPENSER "April," *The Shepheardes Calendar*, 1579

*After an hour of play, the **forswunk** fivesome decides to retire for the night in Mountebank Manor's bevy of beguiling bedchambers.*

QUANKED

KWANKD
adjective

Overcome with fatigue.

Slang; origin unknown.

"I would love to turn a really delightful phrase, be the
wordsmith that makes you commit a line to memory. But
this will have to do for this week. I am quanked."

—MARY ANNE ANDERSEN, "Oh, to Be a Real Wordsmith,"
Iron County Today, 2018

The besotted bouquiniste glimes at the **quanked** *custodian of card catalogs and offers
to share an eiderdown that he surreptitiously swiped.*

SOPOROSE

SAHP-uh-ROHS,
SOH-puh-ROHS

adjective

Characterized by or manifesting an abnormal degree of sleepiness.

Variant of soporous, from Latin *sopor* (sleep) + *-osus* (adjectival suffix).

"The Spirits being oppress'd grow Stupid and
Sluggish, as in Soporose Cases."

—Thomas Fuller, *Pharmacopoeia Extemporanea,* 1710

*The lithesome librarian eyes the shimmering shroud, thinking to herself
that it does seem sumptuously* **soporose** *indeed.*

RAMFEEZLED

ram-FEE-zuhld adjective	**1. Disordered, disturbed, muddled, upset.** **2. Weary, extremely fatigued.** Regional: Scotland, perhaps coined in "Second Epistle to J. Lapraik" by Robert Burns. Origin unknown, perhaps from Scots *ram-* (prefix of intensification), from English slang rum (excellent, fine, great), perhaps from Romani *rom* (husband, man) + Scots *feeze* (to twist, to wriggle) or feeze (to drive off, to defeat).

"He wrocht awa till he was ramfeezled."

—JOHN SERVICE, *Thir Notandums,* 1890

*As radically **ramfeezled** as the beguiling bibliosoph feels, she suspects that, under that eiderdown, neither she nor the bookseller will surrender to slumber anytime soon.*

SOMNIFUGOUS

sahm-NIH-fuh-guhs

adjective

Driving away or preventing sleep, agrypnotic.

From Latin *somnus* (sleep) + *fugare* (to put to flight), from *fuga* (escape, exile) + *-osus* (adjectival suffix).

"'Not all the waters of Lethe could wash such somnifugous tidings from my memory,' replied the butler."

—JANE WEBB, *The Mummy!*, 1827

*The book merchant wonders, with a sly grin, whether the lovable librarian is insinuating that he possesses **somnifugous** properties of which he remains unaware.*

ONEIRODYNIA

OH-neh-roh-DYE-nee-uh

noun

Disturbed imagination during sleep, terrifying dreams, nightmares.

From Ancient Greek ὄνειρος (*óneiros*: dream) + ὀδύνη (*odúnē*: pain, anguish).

"Parr, indeed, in his article 'Mania,' asserts that both constitute nothing more than varieties of one common species; yet with an inconsistency which is too frequently to be met with in his Dictionary, he changes his opinion in the article 'Nosology,' makes *Vesania* the genus, and arranges *melancholia, mania,* and even *oneirodynia* as separate species under it."

—JOHN MASON GOOD, *A Physiological System of Nosology,* 1817

After that fateful night, the bonhomous bouquiniste fears that he or, indeed, all of them might suffer from ominous **oneirodynia** *while asleep.*

DYSANIA

dih-SAY-nee-uh

noun

1. Emotional and/or physical fatigue that causes getting out of bed to be extremely difficult.

2. An overpowering urge to lie back down after getting up.

From Ancient Greek δυσ- (*dus-*: bad, difficult, hard) + ἀνία (*anía*: distress, grief).

"While it's not an official medical diagnosis, dysania can be connected to significant health conditions, so it's important to find out what's going on and how to restore your get-up-and-go."

—from "What Is Dysania?" Healthline.com, 2021

Risking the reputation of a philanderer, the bookseller wants nothing more than a cuddle-compeer with whom to snerdle in a warm bed, **dysania** *be damned.*

SOMNILOQUACIOUS

SAHM-nih-luh-
KWAY-shuhs

adjective

Pertaining to talking or apt to talk during sleep.

From Latin *somnus* (sleep) + *loquax* (talkative), from *loqui* (to speak) + *-ax* (suffix of inclination) + *-osus* (adjectival suffix).

"'Every man his own Freud,' is the cry of the future, and the *Atlantic*, struggling to keep abreast of the foremost files, listens with ears wide open to this tale of somniloquacious augury."

—*ATLANTIC MONTHLY*, 1919

The twitterpated twosome retires for more chitchat and the librarian learns (the hard way) that the lexiphanic bookseller waxes **somniloquacious** *in his sleep.*

HYPNOPOMPIC

HIP-no-PAHM-pik
adjective

Pertaining to the state of partial consciousness just prior to waking.

From Ancient Greek ὕπνος (*húpnos*: sleep) + πομπή (*pompé*: procession), from πέμπειν (*pémpein*: to send) + -ic, from Latin *-icus* (adjectival suffix).

"To similar illusions accompanying the departure of sleep, as when a dream-figure persists for a few moments into waking life, I have given the name hypnopompic."

—FREDERIC MYERS,
Human Personality and Its Survival of Bodily Death, 1903

*The morning concerto of avian arias awakens the disgruntled dapperling, who, sluggishly fighting his **hypnopompic** torpor, whelves his head beneath a blanket.*

EUNEIROPHRENIA

YOO-nih-roh-
FREH-nee-uh

noun

A contented state of mind after waking from a pleasant dream, often accompanied by the desire to return to the dream.

From Ancient Greek εὐ- (*eu-*: good) + ὄνειρος (*óneiros*: dream) + φρήν (*frén*: mind, spirit) + -ία (*-ia*: suffix of abstraction).

"Gynotikolobomassophile (M, 43) seeks neanimorphic F to 60 to share euneirophrenia. Must enjoy pissing off librarians (and be able to provide the correct term for same). Box no. 4732."

— DAVID ROSE, *They Call Me Naughty Lola:*
Personal Ads from the London Review of Books, 2006

Around noon, the langorous librarian, deliciating in **euneirophrenia**, *reluctantly opens one bleary eye to see whether her bedmate still is sleeping soundly.*

EXIPOTIC

ek-sih-PAH-tik

adjective

Purging or cleansing the body of illness, aiding in digestion.

From Hellenistic Greek ἐξιπωτικός (*exipotikós*: purgative), from Ancient Greek ἐξιποῦν (*exipoún*: to squeeze out), from ἐξ- (*ex-*: out of) + ἱποῦν (*ipoún*: to press, to squeeze), from ἵπος (*ipos*: weight, pressure) + -τικός (*-tikós*: adjectival suffix).

"Can a tincture of dogs, of cats, of flowers, of dragons, of inherited treasures, of *stuff*, be exipotic? Or is memory a more reliable antidote?"

— SUE WILLIAM SILVERMAN,
How to Survive Death and Other Inconveniences, 2020

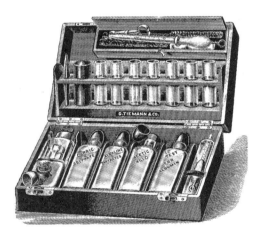

*Sleep has had a remarkably **exipotic** effect on the merry band of bogey busters, who wait while Lady Vellwyn searches the aumbry for coffee.*

UHTCEARE

OOT-kee-AH-ruh	**Predawn anxiety that keeps a person**
noun	**awake and worrying.**

From Old English *uhte* (daybreak) + *ceare* (care, sorrow).

"So best to suffer your uhtceare in silence and wait for the day-raw, which is the first streak of red in the dawn sky."

—MARK FORSYTH, *The Horologicon*, 2012

*Troubling **uhtceare** has spared the librarian and her beau, and the tantalizing aroma of breakfast tempts the twosome from bed at last.*

V

Playful Patois

(TRYSTS & DALLIANCES)

AFFINED

uh-FYND

adjective

1. Joined by affinity or close ties; akin, allied, or confederated.

2. Bound or obligated by affinity or other intimate relation.

From Middle French *affiné* (related, similar), from *affiner* (to enter into a relationship with), from *affin* (spouse, relative by marriage), from Latin *affinis* (connected with), from *ad* (toward) + *finis* (boundary).

"Who shall say what is the invisible tissue—what the innumerable cords—that tie this planet and all its material natures to the millions of worlds with which it is affined?"

—JOHN KENNEDY,
Horse-Shoe Robinson: A Tale of the Tory Ascendency, 1835

Affined by their shared love of recherché tomes and oddball tchotchkes, Paige Penwiper and Baldavin Berggeist realize that it's time to make a matrimonial merger.

VERNALAGNIA

vuhr-nuh-LAG-nee-yuh,
vehr-nuh-LAHN-yuh

noun

A romantic mood that coincides with the departure of cold weather; spring fever.

From Latin *verna* (vernal), from *ver* (the spring season) + *-na* (adjectival suffix) + Ancient Greek λαγνεία (*lagneía*: sexual intercourse), from λαγνεύειν (*lagneúein*: to have sex) + -ία (*-ia*: suffix of abstraction).

"If the events of the past day weren't so horrific, you would feel like having a picnic, a day at the park, or boating; just anything to be outside. For those lovebirds, it was vernalagnia, even though it was the fall season."

—LINDA PHILLIPS,
The Librarian, the Firefighters, and the Arsonist, 2017

*On the leesome spring day of the nuptials, Verbena Vellwyn, serving as the librarian's preeminent paranymph, finds herself in the thrall of vehement **vernalagnia**.*

AMOREVOLOUS

ah-mohr-EH-vuh-luhs

adjective

Loving, kind.

From Italian *amorevole* (loving, affectionate), from Latin *amor* (love) + Italian *-evole* (adjectival suffix), from Latin *-ebilis* + *-osus* (adjectival suffix).

"He would leave it to the princessa to shew her
cordial and amorevolous affections."

—JOHN HACKET,
Bishop Hacket's Memoirs of the Life of Archbishop Williams, 1715

*Giddy with anticipation, the alluring heiress smiles sheepishly, all the love and
romance of weddings making her feel amazingly **amorevolous.***

HALCH

HAHLSH
verb

To clasp, to embrace, to hug.

From halse, from Middle English *halsen* or *halchen*, from Old English *halsian*.

"To halch upon him, King Arthur,
This lady was full faine,
But King Arthur had forgott his lesson,
What he shold say againe."

—from "The Marriage of Sir Gawaine" in *Bishop Percy's Folio*,
edited by John Hales and Frederick Furnivall, c. 1650/1867

*The first time Winter Westhaven saw the bookseller bridegroom and lovestruck librarian **halch**, they knew that the two of them were destined for dreamy devotion.*

LIMERENCE

LIM-uhr-ints noun	**The intoxicating rush of falling in love, accompanied by a tormenting need for requital.**

A neologism coined by psychologist Dorothy Tennov, perhaps influenced by Latin *limen* (threshold, beginning), perhaps from *limus* (sideways, diagonal) + *-men* (nominative suffix) + *-ence*, from Latin *-entia* (suffix of abstraction).

"I first used the term 'amorance' then changed it back to 'limerence.' ... It has no roots whatsoever."

—DOROTHY TENNOV, *The Observer*, 1977

*Relishing the **limerence** of the fiancés, the amorevolous astrologess asks them to recount the sweet story of their enchanting engagement for all assembled.*

ALLANT

GAL-uhnt,
guh-LAHNT

noun, verb

1. A dashing, flirtatious chap who pays excessive attention to women; a suitor, wooer, or seducer.

2. To attend a lady; to convey or escort (a woman); to handle gracefully.

From Middle English *galaunt*, from Old French *galant* (courteous, brave), from *galer* (to make merry, to rejoice), from *gale* (festivity, mirth) + *-ans* (participial suffix).

"When they arrived at their place of destination, Jamaica, Captain Jemmison went on shore to divert himself, and spent his time in great dissipation at Spanish Town, eating, dressing, dancing, gallanting, and glorying in its being observed by all the ladies that he had nothing of a sea-captain about him."

—MARIA EDGEWORTH,
Manoeuvring: Tales of
Fashionable Life, 1809

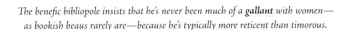
*The benefic bibliopole insists that he's never been much of a **gallant** with women—as bookish beaus rarely are—because he's typically more reticent than timorous.*

OEILLADE

oy-YAHD

noun

A flirty glance or wink.

From Middle French *oeillade*, from *oeil* (eye), from Old French *oil* (modeled on Italian *occhiata*), from Latin *oculus* (eye) + *-ata* (suffix of appearance).

"My devotions proceed no farther than a forenoon's walk,
a sentimental conversation, now and then a squeeze of
the hand or interchanging an oeillade, and when peculiar
good humour and sequestered propriety allow."

—ROBERT BURNS, "Letter to James Dalrymple," 1787

*One auspicious afternoon, the lovable librarian began frequenting the bookseller's
shop, and he eventually espied an occasional* **oeillade** *that kindled a keen interest.*

SPHALLOLALIA

SFAH-loh-LAH-lee-uh

noun

Casually flirtatious chitchat that leads nowhere.

From Ancient Greek σφάλλω (*sfállo*: I kill, I overthrow, I baffle) + λαλιά (*laliá*: talking, chitchat), from λάλος (*lálos*: talkative, loquacious) + -ία (*-ía*: suffix of abstraction).

"Twelve years ago, she would have cracked a joke or teased him with some superfluous sphallolalia just to get a glance of one of his adorably frustrated expressions."

—L Y R A   S A E N Z , *Prelude,* 2 0 2 1

*The twitterpated twosome took to talking, meaningless **sphallolalia** at first, but they discovered that they shared a great quantity of commonalities.*

SMICKER

SMIH-kuhr
verb

To look amorously.

From Middle English *smiker*, from Old English *smicer* (beautiful, elegant).

"Must you be smickering after Wenches while I am in calamity?"

—JOHN DRYDEN, *An Evening's Love*, 1671

*Every time the beatific bibliognost came through the door, the beguiled bookseller sweetly **smickered** at her with one eyebrow roguishly raised.*

PHILOPHOBIA

FIH-luh-FOH-bee-uh

noun

The fear of loving someone or someone loving you.

From Ancient Greek φίλος (*fílos*: dear, beloved) + φόβος (*fóbos*: fear) + -ία (*-ía*: suffix of abstraction).

"We have tried to understand what the causes of different types of philophobia for both men and women are. It was found that the origins are created in the early childhood relationships with their parents."

—ROMINA TAVORMINA, "Why Are We Afraid to Love?," *Psychiatria Danubina*, 26 Suppl. 1, 2014

Neither party suffered from **philophobia**, *but they mutually agreed to carry on cautiously, at an easy pace, sparing themselves the unwanted pressure of rushed expectations.*

TROGLODYTIC

TRAHG-luh-DIH-tik

adjective

1. Of or pertaining to troglodytes or cave dwellers.

2. Characterized by seclusion or reclusive habits.

From Latin *troglodyticus*, from Ancient Greek τρωγλοδυτικός (*troglodutikós*: cave-dwelling), from τρώγλη (*tróglē*: *hole*) + δύειν (*dúein*: to enter, to go into).

"God bless me, the man seems hardly human! Something troglodytic, shall we say? or can it be the old story of Dr. Fell? or is it the mere radiance of a foul soul that thus transpires through, and transfigures, its clay continent?"

—ROBERT LOUIS STEVENSON, *The Strange Case of Dr. Jekyll and Mr. Hyde*, 1886

*Years of reading in solitude and dedication to his profession had rendered the bouquiniste happily **troglodytic**, despite harboring a desire for the flames of redamancy.*

PHILTER

FIHL-tuhr

noun

A drink to arouse desire for a particular person in the drinker, a love potion.

From Middle French *philtre*, from Latin *philtrum*, from Ancient Greek φίλτρον (*fíltron*), from φιλέειν (*filéein*: to love).

"She spoke of philtres and medicated drinks, that in her own country, and in her young days, she had been taught by women learned in the mystery of the art of love, were of potency to inspire corresponding love in the man or maiden, who should drink of them."

—TIMOTHY FLINT, *The Shoshonee Valley*, 1830

The smitten bookseller felt as though the object of his affections had slipped a secret **philter** *into his quotidian cuppa or weekend whiskey.*

AMOURETTE

AH-moo-ret,
ah-moo-RET

noun

An unsatisfying love affair or one of little consequence, a dalliance.

From French *amourette*, from *amour*, from Latin *amor* (love) + French *-ette* (diminutive suffix), from Medieval Latin *-ittus*, from Latin *-itus* (adjectival suffix).

"Edward IV had, with many great Qualifications, some very considerable Failings; he was immoderately addicted to his Pleasures, especially to Amourettes and Intrigues with Women."

—PATRICK ABERCROMBY,
The Martial Atchievements of the Scots Nation, 1715

*Because the merchant wanted no ambiguous **amourette**, by the time the business with that baronial biblioklept began, he was seeking something more substantial.*

REDAMANCY

REH-*duh-muhn-see*

noun

Mutual love, love requited.

From Latin *redamantia*, from *redamare* (to return love), coined by Roman statesman and orator Marcus Tullius Cicero, from *red-*, variant of *re-* (responsive, again) + *amare* (to love).

"Redamancy is distinguished from most of the other words about love in that it is one of the few that specifies reciprocity."

—AMMON SHEA, *Reading the OED*, 2008

*The fetching fashionista muses that **redamancy**, the harrowing hole of limerence filled, remains a rewarding rarity among the bookish classes.*

EROTOGRAPHOMANIA

ehr-AH-toh-GRAF-oh-MAY-nee-uh

noun

1. An immoderate degree of fascination with erotic literature.

2. A sexual compulsion or obsession with writing love letters or poems.

From Ancient Greek ἔρωτος (*érotos*), genitive of ἔρως (*éros*: love) + γραφή (*graphé*: writing) + μανία (*manía*: madness).

"There exists also a comparatively blameless, more or less physiological, erotographomania of the time of puberty, in which most passionate letters are written to imaginary lovers, and the still obscure sexual impulse finds a satisfaction in these erotic imaginations."

—IWAN BLOCH,
The Sexual Life of Our Time in Its Relation to Modern Civilization,
translated by M. Eden Paul, 1914

After the momentous night at Mountebank Manor, a curious case of **erotographomania** *besotted the beguiled bouquiniste, who promptly sharpened all his nibs at once.*

HONEYFUGGLE

HUH-nee-FUH-guhl
verb

To pay someone a compliment in order to get something; to flatter, cajole, or blandish.

Regional: America. From honey, from Middle English *hony*, from Old English *hunig* + *fugle* (to maneuver, to manipulate).

"'Oh, you hypocrite! You can't honeyfuggle me—'
Gurgle, gurgle, gurgle, the champagne
flowed down her throat.
'Honeyfuggle *you*? Oh, you
bewitching creature, *you* honeyfuggle
me! Another glass, Fontaine.'"

—MOLLY ELLIOT SEAWELL,
*The Sprightly Romance
of Marsac*, 1896

*The besotted bookman hid his lightly lascivious love letters about the shop, and the
playful polyhistor made a game of **honeyfuggling** clues as to their whereabouts.*

169

SOFT-SOAP

SAHFT-sohp

verb

To soothe or persuade with flattery or codswallop.

From soft, from Middle English *softe*, from Old English *sôfte*, from *sêfte* + soap, from Middle English *sope*, from Old English *sape* (soap, salve).

"'Hearing this,' pursued Hickory, answering the look of impatience in the other's face, 'I had a curiosity to interview the observatory, and being—well, not a clumsy fellow at softsoaping a girl—I at last succeeded in prevailing upon her to take me up.'"

—ANNA KATHARINE GREEN, *Hand and Ring*, 1883

The designer, an incorrigible romantic, thinks a scavenger hunt for billets-doux an ideal means for besotted bibliophiles to **soft-soap** *each other.*

GAMOMANIA

gam-oh-MAY-nee-uh

noun

1. An obsession with marriage.

2. Insanity characterized by the compulsion to make outlandish marriage proposals.

From Ancient Greek γάμος (*gámos:* marriage, matrimony) + μανία (*manía:* madness).

"The fiery trial under Mary, and the slights which Elizabeth never failed to put upon the wives of clergymen, although she wisely did not allow her prejudice *inevitably* to stop the preferment of their husbands, may have done something to abate this gamomania: poverty did more."

—from "The Parsonage," *British Magazine and Monthly Register,* 1841

Aflutter with **gamomania**, *the book merchant popped the question by means of a stratospheric scrivener and a flashmob of flatulists.*

LEMAN

LEH-muhn

noun

1. A dear or beloved person, a sweetheart.

2. A mistress or paramour (disparaging).

From Middle English *lefman*, from *liefman*, from Old English *lēof* (dear, beloved) + *mann* (man, person).

"Then like a Faerie knight him selfe he drest;
For every shape on him he could endew:
Then like a king he was to her exprest,
And offered kingdoms unto her in view,
To be his Leman and his Lady trew."

—EDMUND SPENSER, *The Faerie Queene*, 1590

*The haute couture haberdasher wonders, with a wink and a nudge, whether Oswin Otterbuck has some mysterious **leman** squirreled away, of which the coterie is unaware.*

DOWSABEL

DAU-suh-behl

noun

A female sweetheart or ladylove.

From the proper name, perhaps from Middle English or French *douce et belle* (soft and beautiful), from Old French *dous*, from Latin *dulcis* (sweet) + *et* (and) + *bella*.

"'To Adriana!' that is where we dined,
Where Dowsabel did claim me for her husband."

—WILLIAM SHAKESPEARE, *The Comedy of Errors*, 1594/1623

The wheedling wangler throws fuel on the fire, musing that the conservator could have a delitescent **dowsabel** *whom he sends on scavenger hunts for mawkish missives.*

SUPPALPATION

suh-puhl-PAY-shuhn

noun

The act of enticing by soft words, an enticement.

From Medieval Latin *suppalpatio* (flattery), from Latin *suppalpari* (to coax, to wheedle), from *sub* (under, beneath) + *palpari* (to be patted, to be stroked) + *-tio* (nominative suffix).

"Thou art a Courtier, and hast laid a plot to rise: if obsequious servility to the great, if those gifts in the bosom which our blunt ancestors would have termed bribes, if plausible suppalpations, if restless importunities will noise thee, thou wilt mount: but something there is, that clogs thy heel, or blocks thy way."

—BISHOP JOSEPH HALL, *The Shaking of the Olive-Tree*, 1641

*The wedding party's sly and suppositious **suppalpation** is going nowhere, but they continue cajoling the pensive pedagogue.*

DULCINEA

duhl-SIH-nee-yuh, *DOOL-sih-NAY-uh*	**A mistress, a ladylove, a sweetheart.**
noun	From the character Dulcinea del Toboso in *Don Quixote* by Miguel de Cervantes y Saavedra. From Spanish *dulce* (sweet), from Latin *dulcis* + *-ina* (adjectival suffix).

"'Tis not Venus' picture that, nor the Spanish Infanta's, as you suppose (good sir), no Princesse, or Kings daughter: no, no, but his divine mistris, forsooth, his dainty Dulcinia, his deare Antiphila, to whose service he is wholly consecrate, whom he alone adores."

—ROBERT BURTON, *Anatomy of Melancholy*, 1624

*Because he never goes about arm in arm with some delightful **dulcinea**, could the charming chap be a committed bachelor disinclined to courtship?*

TUTOYANT

TOO-*twoy-ohn,*
too-twoy-AHN(T)

adjective

Affectionate, familiar, intimate.

From French *tutoyant* (familiar), from *tutoyer* (to be familiar with, to address informally), from *tu* (thou, second person singular), from Latin *tu* + French *-oyer* (verbal suffix), from Old French *-oier*, from Latin *-idiare*.

"He brutalizes the holier familiarities of home life; turns facile and covert scorn upon the pretty tutoyant affection of happily wedded woman and man, suggests feverish sin as a result of perfect matrimonial union, and does this graceless favor with the subtlety of an Iago."

—AMY LESLIE, *Some Players*, 1899

The gallant guardian of gilded Greek goblets secretly is smitten with a special someone, and would like to become even more **tutoyant** *with said individual.*

INNERLY

IHN-*uhr-lee*

adjective

Of persons: affectionate, compassionate.

Regional: Scotland. From Scots *innerlie*, from Old English *innera*, comparative of *inne* (within) + *-lic* (adjectival suffix).

"So mature, so large, and so innerly was his knowledge, that after his death, letters of sorrow came from the Continent, and elsewhere, indicating that he was considered twice his real age."

—JOHN BROWN,
John Leech and Other Papers/Horae Subsecivae, 1866

Each feels **innerly** *toward the other, but neither knows that they share that same depth and fervency of feeling.*

DRUERY

(also: drury, drewery)

DROO-ree,
DROO-uhr-ee

noun

1. Love, gallantry, affection.

2. A love token or gift, especially a jewel or other precious object.

3. A mistress.

From Old French *druerie* (love, friendship), from *dru* (friend) + *-erie*, from Latin *-arius* (suffix of agency).

"He gaif hir ane lufe drowrie,
Ane Ring set with
ane riche Rubie."

—DAVID LYNDSAY,
*The Historie and Testament
of Squyer Meldrum,* 1594

*A patient man, the self-styled savior of superannuated souvenirs plays the long game, having resigned himself to contentment with whatever **druery** he receives.*

PARANYMPH

PEHR-uh-nimf

noun

1. In Ancient Greece, the friend who accompanied the groom when he brought home his bride.

2. A groomsman, best man, bridesmaid, or maid of honor.

3. Someone who gives countenance and support to another, a wingman.

From Middle French *paranymphe*, from Latin *paranymphus*, from Ancient Greek παράνυμφος (*paránumfos*: a bridegroom's friend), from παρα- (*para-*: around) + νύμφη (*númfē*: bride).

"I hope she is by this time Lady Creswell, and that my sweet little Harriet had the pleasure and honour of being her paranymph."

—ELIZABETH GRIFFITH, *The History of Lady Barton*, 1771

*At long last, the nuptials commence, and the connubial coordinatrice prompts the **paranymphs** to proceed to their appointed places.*

BLITHESOME

BLYTH-suhm

adjective

Joyous, happy, cheerful.

From blithe (cheerful, happy), from Old English *bliþe* (gentle, happy) + -some (adjectival suffix of significance), from Middle English *-som*, from Old English *-sum*.

"Speak gently to the herring, and kindly to the calf,
Be blithesome with the bunny, at barnacles don't laugh!"

—JOSEPH ASHBY-STERRY,
"A SECULAR SERMON," *The Lazy Minstrel*, 1886

The officiant counterposes this **blithesome** *handfasting to last week's hymeneal hubbleshoo, during which an infidelity flung the feculence into the flabellum.*

PIGSNEY

(also: pigsny)
PIHGZ-nee

noun

1. A term of endearment for a beloved woman or girl.

2. A darling, a sweetheart.

From Middle English *piggesnye* (a pig's eye), from *pigges* (genitive of pig) + *nye*, from *an (e)ye*.

"Hir shoes were laced on hir legges hye;
She was a prymerole, a piggesnye,
For any lord to leggen in his bedde."

—GEOFFREY CHAUCER,
"The Miller's Tale,"
The Canterbury Tales, c. 1400

From an antechamber rises a risibly reproachful reprimand: "Yes, I love you, too, darling, but if you call me 'pigsney' again, we're curtains, buster!"

GLIME

GLEIM	**A sidelong look, a glance askance.**
noun	
	Regional: Scotland. From Scots *glime*, origin unknown, perhaps from Old Scots *glim* (glance, glimpse).

"'Aw, ye wouldn't think it's true, would ye, now?' said
Ned, with a wink at Dan and a 'glime' at Davy."

—HALL CAINE, *The Deemster*, 1887

The ceremonial strategist, displaying the disingenuous dentition of an eccedentesiast,
*gives the groom a grinning **glime** and launches him toward the altar.*

BASOREXIA

BAH-zoh-REK-see-uh

noun

The overpowering urge or desire to kiss someone.

From Latin *basiare* (to kiss) + *orexis* (hunger, longing), from Ancient Greek ὄρεξις (*órexis*: desire), from ὀρέγειν (*orégein*: to reach, to stretch).

"Looks like they're having a bad case of basorexia."

—LINDSEY ROSIN, *Cherry*, 2016

*Brimming with **basorexia**, the brunettish bride and grizzled groom want the ceremony's magic to last forever but are impatient to get to the kissing part.*

PROTHALAMIUM

PROH-thuh-LAY-
mee-uhm,

PROH-thuh-LAH-
mee-uhm

noun

A song or poem to celebrate a wedding.

From "Prothalamion," a poem by Edmund Spenser
celebrating the double marriage of two daughters
of Edward Somerset, 4th Earl of Worcester, from
Ancient Greek πρό (*pró*: for) + θάλαμος (*thálamos*:
wedding chamber) + *-ιον* (*-ion*: suffix of location).

"There, again, we listen to the litany of the Muses . . . or else hear the
fairy prothalamium, most irrepressible and inimitable of bridal songs."

—WALTER GREG, *Pastoral Poetry and Pastoral Drama*, 1906

*A shimmering chanteuse intones a pleasuresome **prothalamium**, and the grand
ceremony commences with the playing of Mendelssohn's "Hochzeitsmarsch."*

⊰ TROTH ⊱

TROHTH noun	**1. Truth, verity.**
	2. Faith, fidelity.
	From Middle English *trothe*, variant of *treuth* (fidelity, oath, truth), from Old English *trēowþ* (faith, pledge, truth).

"The Troth was pledged in a few high-priced Trinkets
which she had decided upon before he spoke to her."

—GEORGE ADE, *Ade's Fables*, 1914

Bride and groom joyously plight their **troth**, *one to the other, always and forever,*
with vows made and coruscant rings exchanged to seal the deal.

SMEERIKIN

SMIHR-ih-kin | **An intensely passionate or stolen kiss.**

noun

Regional: Scotland. From Scots *smuirich* (to kiss, to caress), from *smuir* (to smother with kisses) + *-ich* (suffix of intensification) + *-in* (dimunitive suffix).

"Few joys on earth exceed a smeerikin."

—JOHN MACTAGGART,
The Scottish Gallovidian Encyclopedia, 1824

Their hands bound together, the groom leans forward, planting a crackerjack of a **smeerikin** *upon the eager lips of his newly trothed bride.*

OSCULATION

ahs-kyoo-LAY-shuhn

noun

A kiss, kissing.

From Latin *osculatio* (a kiss), from *osculari* (to kiss, to embrace) + *-tio* (nominative suffix).

"When the children departed after an orgy of osculation, Jaffery surveyed with a twinkling eye the decorous quartette sitting by the fire."

—William Locke, *Jaffery*, 1915

The bookish bridal couple hold their Orphic **osculation** *in a magical moment of matrimonial mansuetude while all in attendance stand to cheer the joyous occasion.*

CATAGLOTTISM

KA-tuh-GLAH-tiz-um

noun

Kissing with tongue, French kissing.

From French *cataglottisme*, from Ancient Greek καταγλώττισμα (*kataglóttisma*: a lascivious kiss), from κατά (*katá*: downward) + γλῶττα (*glôtta*: tongue).

"The kiss is not only an expression of feeling; it is a means of provoking it. Cataglottism is by no means confined to pigeons."

—HAVELOCK ELLIS,
Studies in the Psychology of Sex, volume 4, 1905

So as not to discomfit their darling guests, the newlyweds disentwine before the concupiscent call of **cataglottism** *can consume them.*

A · B · C · D · E · F · G · H · I · J · K · L · M

VI

JOLLY
JUBILATIONS

(HAPPINESS & CELEBRATION)

N · O · P · Q · R · S · T · U · V · W · X · Y · Z

ECSTASIATE

ek-STAY-see-ayt
verb

To (cause to) go into ecstasy, to become ecstatic, to give pleasurable excitement.

From French *extasier* (to go into ecstasy), from Middle French *extasie*, from Old French *estaise*, from Latin *ecstasis*, from Ancient Greek ἔκστασις (*ékstasis*), from ἐξιστάναι (*existánai*: to displace), from ἐκ (*ek*: out) + ἱστάναι (*histánai*: to stand) + -ate (verbal suffix), from Latin *-atus*.

"He was a perfect original; of course he 'had served,' and equally of course, he extasiated on the Emperor, and shrugged his shoulders at all other crowned heads, past, present, and to come."

—JULIA PARDOE,
The River and the Desert, 1838

Prudery is patently patronizing, particularly at the wedding of wordsmiths, so Baldavin Berggeist and Paige Penwiper **ecstasiate** *the crowd with another kiss before jumping the broom.*

REVERDIE

ruh-VEHR-dee,
REH-vuhr-dee

noun

A poem, song, or dance that celebrates the return of spring.

From Old French *reverdie* (foliage, verdure), from *reverdier* (to become green again), from *re-* (again) + *verdier* (to grow green), from Latin *viridis* (green) + French *-er* (verbal suffix), from Latin *-are*.

"For, by and by, he spun a languid lay
Set her a weeping for an April day.
And then a reverdie, I scarcely knew
Just what it meant; by times the damsel grew
Pensive and tender, till at last she said,—
You see the bait was very nicely spread,—
'How chances it, fair sir, this gift of song
Lay thus unused?'"

—SILAS WEIR MITCHELL,
"François Villon,"
Collected Poems, 1896

*The reception commences with an idyllist reciting a radiant **reverdie**, after which the gallivanting guests go 'round the maypole, singing ancient songs of fecundity.*

WEAL

WEEL	1. Wealth, riches.
noun	2. Prosperity, success.
	3. Happiness, well-being.

From Middle English *wele*, from Old English *wela*.

"Father can await his boy's final clearance from guilty
suspicions in patient abeyance to public weal."

—CARSON JAY LEE, *Oswald Langdon*, 1900

*The bridegroom's brother gives the happy couple an auspicious toast,
wishing them a wellspring of **weal** for all their days to come.*

CONJUBILANT

kuhn-JOO-bih-luhnt
adjective

Pertaining to shouting or singing together joyously or cheering as a group.

From Medieval Latin *conjubilare*, from Latin *cum* (with) + *iubilare* (to cheer, to shout joyfully).

"They stand, those halls of Syon,
Conjubilant with song,
And bright with many an angel,
And all the martyr throng."

—BERNARD OF CLUNY, "The Celestial Country,"
translated by John Mason Neale, 1100S/1867

ONE A.M AT THE CAFÉ VACHETTE

In response to the warmhearted wedding toast, the banquet hall erupts in a **conjubilant** *cacophony of huzzahs and hear, hears!*

LOBDOCIOUS

lob-DOH-shuhs

adjective

1 Delightful, excellent.

2 Delicious, tasty, sapid, scrummy.

Regional: America. Slang, perhaps influenced by love, from Middle English *luve*, from Old English *lufu* + braggadocious (boastful), from Braggadocchio, a character in Edmund Spenser's *The Faerie Queene*, from braggard (a boaster), from Middle English *braggen* (to shout, to boast) + *-ard*, from Old French *-ard* (suffix of significance) + Italian *occhio* (eye), from Latin *oculus*.

"This pie is lobdocious."

—ELSIE WARNOCK, *Dialect Notes*, 1917

Fascinated by the flotilla of fancy finger food floating her way, the bride's sister-in-law declares all the delicacies to be **lobdocious.**

TRIPUDIATE

trih-PYOO-dee-ayt

verb

To dance for celebration or joy.

From Latin *tripudiare* (to dance, to cavort, to leap about).

"The Earth did rejoice and tripudiate when the Saviour came forth alive out of the belly of the Grave."

—JOHN HACKET, *A Century of Sermons*, 1670

*The time comes to **tripudiate**, so the gamboling gramophonist, who has erected his equipage upon the rosewood rostrum, means to make with the madcap melodies.*

GEMÜTLICH

guh-MOOT-lik,
guh-MYOOT-likh

adjective

1. Cozy, homely, pleasant.

2. Cheerful, good-natured.

From German *gemütlich*, from Middle High German *gemüetlich*, from *gemüet* (mind, mentality), from Old High German *muot* (courage, spirit) + German *-lich* (adjectival suffix), from Old High German *-lih*.

"The view was so beautiful over the dear hills; the
day so fine; the whole so gemüthlich."

—QUEEN VICTORIA, "Monday, October 11, 1852,"
Leaves from the Journal of Our Life in the Highlands, 1868

Ebullient with anticipation, all in the hall gaze with **gemütlich** *glee as the groom
leads the bride for their debut dance: a pasodoble (interesting choice).*

QUEME

(also: queem)	**1. Comfortable, enjoyable, pleasant.**
KWEEM	
adjective, verb	**2. To please.**

From Middle English *quemen* (to please), from Old English *cwēman* (to gratify, to satisfy).

"And Amphion that hath suche excellence
Of musyke ay dyde his besynes
To plese and queme Venus the goddesse."

—JOHN LYDGATE, *The Temple of Glass*, 1477

Day turns to night, and the brass horns of the mix-maestro's double gramophones make melodies most **queme** *that conjure corybantic capering on the dance floor.*

WUZZLE

WUH-zuhl
verb

To mingle, mix, or muddle.

Regional: America. Origin unknown.

"Wal, the upshot on't was, they fussed and fuzzled and wuzzled
till they'd drinked up all the tea in the teapot; and then they went
down and called on the parson, and wuzzled him all up talkin'
about this, that, and t'other that wanted lookin' to, and that it
was no way to leave everything to a young chit like Huldy, and
that he ought to be lookin' about for an experienced woman."

—HARRIET BEECHER STOWE, *The Minister's Wooing*, 1859

*Suffonsified from the sumptuous nuptial repast, the wedding guests **wuzzle** merrily
about the hall in search of delightsome divertissements.*

POCULATION

PAHK-yoo-LAY-shun

noun

The drinking of alcohol.

From Latin *poculum* (cup, tankard), from Old Latin *poclum* + Latin *-atio*, variant of *-tio* (nominative suffix).

"The art of poculation, if so it may be termed, being of the highest antiquity, and the claims of Bacchus as the *inventor* of the art being unquestioned."

— D. C., "Signs of the Times,"
New Monthly Magazine and Humorist, 1837

A lavishly gilded sign imprinted with those two most magical of words—
"open bar"—prompts the **poculation** *to continue apace.*

FRABJOUS

FRAB-jus adjective	**Fabulous, fair, and joyous.**
	A nonce word coined in "Jabberwocky" by Lewis Carroll.

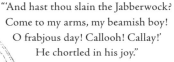

"'And hast thou slain the Jabberwock?
Come to my arms, my beamish boy!
O frabjous day! Callooh! Callay!'
He chortled in his joy."

—LEWIS CARROLL,
"Jabberwocky" 1871

*"I'm so invited that I was delighted!" says one potation-partaking
paranymph of the fantastically **frabjous** day.*

SNUGGERY

SNUH-guhr-ee
noun

A snug or warm and comfortable place, as a small room.

From snug (tight, handsome), perhaps from Old Norse *snøggr* (fast, quick) + -ery (suffix of location), from Middle English *-erie*, from French *-ier* (suffix of profession), from Latin *-arius* (suffix of agency).

"'So now, my dear,' Zeluca characteristically expressed herself, 'my sage mama is willing to allow her precipitate daughter is right in saying it was monstrous in your family to enjoin you such rigid seclusions; and she joins me, in saying you must come and dine, and sleep with us to—play whist in a snuggerie with Lady Whitelock!'"

—ANONYMOUS, *Zeluca*, 1815

*After several dizzying dances, a squiffy squadron of giggling guests hie themselves to a secluded **snuggery** to discalceate and dish.*

LUDIC

LOO-dik

adjective

Pertaining to impromptu, unguided playfulness.

From French *ludique* (playful), from Latin *ludere* (to play), from *ludus* (game, sport) + Old French *-ique*, from Latin *-icus* (adjectival suffix).

"I lied and fantasized and deceived; my existence, too, was a prismatic web of mendacity—but for me it was far more—what?—far more ludic, literary, answering an intellectual rather than an emotional need."

—MARTIN AMIS, *The Rachel Papers*, 1973

*Guests take a **ludic** lap about the vast venue, playing a decidedly debauched version of Lemur in the Gyre.*

SITOOTERIE

(also: sitootery)

sih-TOO-tuhr-ee

noun

1. A lovely outdoor place to sit and relax, such as a gazebo or patio.

2. A quiet corner to sit out a dance with your partner.

Regional: Scotland. From sit, from Middle English *sitten*, from Old English *sittan* + Scots *oot* (out), from Old English *ut* (outside) + -ery (suffix of location), from Middle English -*erie*, from French -*ier* (suffix of profession), from Latin -*arius* (suffix of agency).

"The Reid Hall was suitably rigged up in unwonted 'braws,' the 'Sitooterie' especially being voted a great success, while the platform was adorned by pot plants and Mr. Kydd's orchestra."

—from "The Drummer," *Forfar Dispatch*, 1920

*In the garden **sitooterie**, a motley troupe of musicians plays a more tribal style of music than the vinyl virtuoso is spinning indoors.*

DISPORT

diss-POHRT verb	**To play, to indulge in gaiety.**
	From Middle English *disporten* (to partake in amusement), from Old French *desporter*, from Latin *deportare* (to bring, to convey, to banish), from *de-* (from, off) + *portare* (to bear, to carry).

"From the twentieth houre you shall see none at all in their shops: for then every man runs to the Taverne to disport, to spend riotously, and to be drunken."

—SAMUEL PURCHAS, *Hakluytus Posthumus*, 1905

Dexterous drumming draws a festively festooned flock, who dance around the percussionists, **disporting** *in unbridled (well, slightly bridled) frivolity.*

ALLEGRESSE

al-uh-GRESS

noun

Cheerfulness, elation, joy.

From French *allégresse* (gladness), from *allègre* (happy, joyful), from Old French *halaigre*, from Latin *alacris*, genitive of *alacer* (brisk, sprightly) + French *-esse*, from Old French *-ece*, from Latin *-itia*, variant of *-ia* (suffix of abstraction).

"I went up to the dancers, hoping to see that real gaiety and allegresse in all their motions—that unaffected unspoiled beauty and grace in their persons, which one is told is only to be met with in the native dances of peasants, and in comparison with which our beauties in ball-rooms are cold and insipid."

—MARY BERRY, *Extracts of the Journals and Correspondence of Miss Berry*, 1865

*An all-encompassing **allegresse** permeates the atmosphere, and everyone is in the highest of spirits . . . well, almost everyone.*

INKLE

ING-kuhl

noun, verb

1. A narrow strip of decorative fabric used as trimming.

2. To join a gathering to which one has no invitation, to crash a party.

Origin unknown, perhaps from lingel (cobbler's thread, a small strip of leather), from French *ligneul*, from Latin *linea* (linen thread, a physical line), from *linum* (flax). The figurative use of the verb comes from 1920s flapper slang.

"When people are intimate, we say they are as great as two inkle-weavers, on which expression I have to remark in the first place, that the word *great* is here used in a sense which the corresponding term has not, so far as I know, in any other language—and secondly, that inkle-weavers contract intimacies with each other sooner than other people, on account of their juxtaposition in weaving of inkle."

—WILLIAM COWPER,
"To Lady Hesketh,"
MAY 6, 1788

*The late baron's henchman, a blundering blaggard if ever there was one, preposterously presumes that he can **inkle** his way into the reception sans invite.*

ANTITHALIAN

an-tih-THAY-lee-uhn adjective	**Opposed to fun or festivity.**

From anti-, from Ancient Greek ἀντι- (*anti-*: against) + thalian (comic, comedic), from Ancient Greek Θαλία (*Thalía*, one of the three Graces; the muse of comedy and idyllic poetry; and one of the 50 Nereids), from Ancient Greek θάλλειν (*thállein*: to bloom, to flourish) + -an, from Old French -*ain*, from Latin -*anus* (adjectival suffix).

"She was finishing her education in a German convent, but Mr. Toobad described her as being fully impressed with the truth of his Ahrimanic philosophy, and being altogether as gloomy and antithalian a young lady as Mr. Glowry himself could desire for the future mistress of Nightmare Abbey."

—THOMAS LOVE PEACOCK, *Nightmare Abbey*, 1818

*The **antithalian** interloper blends with the tribe of levitous literati almost as well as a cantankerous camel crashing a flamboyance of flamingos.*

NIKHEDONIA

nee-kay-DOH-nee-uh

noun

The enjoyment or pleasure of anticipating victory or success.

From Ancient Greek νίκη (*níkē*: victory) + ἡδονή (*hēdoné*: pleasure), from ἡδύς (*hēdús*: sweet) + -ία (*-ía*: suffix of abstraction).

"It is just trading. Take the emotion out of it. Get the nikhedonia session over with before you trade."

—NEAL WEINTRAUB, *Tricks of the Active Trader,* 2006

Filled with overhasty **nikhedonia,** *the ninnyhammer plans to ingratiate himself with Lord Mitherton, whom he unwittingly had abducted on the promenade.*

DESIPIENCE

duh-SIH-pee-ints

noun

Dillydallying, nonsense, silliness, trifling.

From Latin *desipientia* (folly, silliness), from *desipere* (to be foolish), from *de* (from) + *sapere* (to know, to understand).

"The author's humour is certainly not one which eschews simple in favour of subtle means, or which is averse from occasional desipience in the form of the wildest farce."

—ADOLPHUS WARD, *Dickens*, 1882

*Distracted by his own **desipience**, the henchman masticates myriad munchables, heedless that the newlyweds have gone to the train station.*

DELICIATE

duh-LISS-ee-ayt

verb

To indulge or delight in something enjoyable.

From Latin *delicia* (delight, pleasure), from *delicere* (to allure, to entice), from *de* (away) + *lacere* (to lure, to deceive) + *-atus* (verbal suffix).

"That their very Bodies were Nourished by the Vapours and Fumes, arising from them; and that these Evil Demons therefore did as it were Deliciate and Epicurize in them."

—RALPH CUDWORTH,
The True Intellectual System of the Universe: The First Part, 1678

Deliciating *in devils on horseback, the blaggard perceives an almond in the Stilton and, his weasand constricting, crashes through the sideboard.*

GRAMERCY

gruh-MUHR-see	**An exclamation of gratitude.**
interjection	

From Middle English *gramerci*, from Old French *gran(t) merci* (great thanks), from Latin *grandis* (great, large) + *merces* (wages, revenue), from *merx* (goods, merchandise).

"'Now, thanks, my loving Uncle,' that Lady gay replied;
'Gramercy for thy benison!'—then 'Out, alas!' she sighed;
'My father dear he is not near; he seeks the Spanish Main;
He prays thee give me shelter here till he return again!'"

—RICHARD HARRIS BARHAM, *The Ingoldsby Legends*, 1842

*Sprawled amid shards of crystal and crockery, the man opens his eyes—as an apothecary releases the valve of his trusty sphygmomanometer—and cries "**Gramercy!**"*

211

EUDAEMONIA

(also: eudemonia)
yoo-duh-MOH-nee-uh

noun

A peaceful sense of contentment, a state of happiness, joy, or well-being.

From Ancient Greek εὐδαιμονία (*eudaimonia*: happiness, well-being), from εὐ- (*eu-*: good) + δαίμων (*daimon*: spirit, soul) + -ία (-*ia*, suffix of abstraction).

"The fundamental difficulty which confronts those who would distinguish between pleasure and eudaemonia is that all pleasure is ultimately a mental phenomenon, whether it be roused by food, music, doing a moral action or committing a theft."

—from "Eudaemonism," *Encyclopaedia Britannica*, 1911

*Suffused with uncharacteristic **eudaemonia** after narrowly escaping death amandine, the lubberly lummox decides to dedicate his life to philanthropic pursuits.*

ATARAXY

A-tuh-RAK-see

noun

A state of being undisturbed, imperturbed, or indifferent.

From Middle French *ataraxie*, from Ancient Greek ἀταραξία (*ataraxía*: impassiveness), from ἀ- (*a-*: not) + ταράσσειν (*tarássein*: to agitate, to disturb).

"He was not handsome, he was not young, he was not rich; he was not sad, because his wisdom approached the happy state of ataraxy, without, however, finally attaining it, and he was not glad, because he was somewhat of a sensualist, and his soul was not free from illusions and desires."

—ANATOLE FRANCE, *The Amethyst Ring*,
translated by Frederic Chapman, 1899/1919

*Vowing to eschew **ataraxy**, the henchman sells all his belongings, donates the money to fund food allergy research, and joins a priory, after which he is never heard from again.*

RUSTICATE

RUS-tih-kayt

verb

1. To live in the countryside.

2. To go or send to the countryside.

3. As a punishment, to compel a student back to the boonies as a suspension from college or university.

From rustic (rural), from Latin *rusticus* (rural, rough, simple), from *rus* (fields, farm, village) + *-tus* (adjectival suffix) + *-icus* (adjectival suffix) + *-ate* (verbal suffix), from Latin *-atus*.

"We are here bless'd with the benign and comfortable Rays of a glorious Sun, breathing a free and wholesome Air, without the noisome Smell of stinking Fogs or other malignant Fumes and Vapours, too common in large Cities; especially where they are situated near navigable Rivers, or the Sea; which is the reason that numbers of Citizens are obliged to rusticate very often, to avoid the necessary Stagnation, and Fermentation of such variety of all."

—JOHN SOAME,
Hampstead Wells, 1734

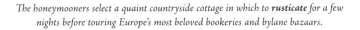

The honeymooners select a quaint countryside cottage in which to **rusticate** *for a few nights before touring Europe's most beloved bookeries and bylane bazaars.*

INCABINATE

ihn-KA-bih-nayt verb	**1. To enclose in a cabin or cabinet.**
	2. To confine or restrict.

From in + cabin, from Middle English *caban*, from Old French *cabane*, from Medieval Latin *capanna*, from Latin *cabanna* (hut) + -ate (verbal suffix), from Latin -atus.

"This power was incabinated within the breast
of Emperours, Kings and Generals."

—THOMAS VENN, *Military and Maritime Discipline*, 1672

*After the hoopla and hullabaloo, the bookish couple **incabinate** themselves
in a cozy little cottage for some much-needed rest and relaxation.*

GAUDEAMUS

goh-dee-AY-muhs,
GAU-dee-AH-muhs

noun

A humdinger of a party, particularly one thrown by students.

From Latin *gaudeamus* (let us rejoice), from *gaudere* (to rejoice, to enjoy).

"Our Bannatyne Club goes on *à merveille*, only that at our *gaudeamus* this year we drank our wine *more majorum*, and our new judge, Lord Eldin, had a bad fall on the staircase, which has given rise to some bad jokes, as for instance, that to match Coke upon Littleton we have got Eldin upon Stair, and so forth."

—WALTER SCOTT, "To John Richardson,"
Familiar Letters of Sir Walter Scott, volume 2, 1823/1894

The full moon rises as the connubial festivities conclude, but a clamorous
gaudeamus *startles the couple from their serene repose.*

SHIVAREE

SHIV-uh-ree noun	**1. A clamorous, clanging performance, often on pots and pans, by people gathered to celebrate a wedding.**
	2. A tumultuous commotion or uproar.

From sherrie-varrie, from French *charivari*, from Old French *chalivali* (noise made with pots and pans), from Medieval Latin *caribaria* (headache), from Latin *carivaria*, from Ancient Greek καρηβάρεια (*karēbáreia*), from κάρη (*kárē*: head) + βαρύς (*barús*: heavy).

"So in blind desperation I started such a rattling 'shivaree' down below as never had astounded an engineer in this world before, I fancy. Amidst the frenzy of the bells the engines began to back and fill in a furious way, and my reason forsook its throne."

—MARK TWAIN, *Life on the Mississippi*, 1883

*A carousing crowd, hearing that newlyweds are staying at the cottage, commences a lollapalooza of a **shivaree** for their honeymoon.*

GILRAVAGE

gil-RAV-ihj verb	**To guzzle and devour, to indulge in noisy, riotous jollity.** Regional: Scotland. Origin unknown, perhaps from Scots *gil-* (prefix of intensification) + ravage, from French *ravage* (to despoil, to ruin), from Old French *ravir* (to ravish, to plunder), from Latin *rapere* (to seize, to snatch).

"At all former and precedent banquets, it had been the custom to give vent to muckle wanton and luxurious indulgence, and to galravitch, both at hack and manger, in a very expensive manner to the funds of the town."

—JOHN GALT, *The Provost*, 1822

*Hoping for uneventful peace and languorous quiet, neither the bouquiniste bridegroom nor the bibliosoph bride cares to **gilravage** (yet again).*

CALLITHUMPIAN

kal-ih-THUHMP-ee-in
adjective

Discordantly noisy like a gathering or parade of rowdy celebrants.

Regional: America. From gallithumpian (a disturber of order during eighteenth-century British elections), from gally (to frighten, to worry), from gallow (to scare, to terrify), from Middle English [*galowen*] *begalewen* (to [be]gallow), from Old English [*gælwian*] *agælwed* (to surprise[d], to perturb[ed]) + thump (onomatopoetic) + -ian, from Latin -ianus (adjectival suffix).

"The call lasts ten or fifteen minutes, and occasionally has the accompaniment of callithumpian discord, blended with the fiendish screeches of a dozen frenzied locomotives."

—RICHARD WHEATLEY, "The New York Produce Exchange," *Harper's Magazine,* 1886

*The **callithumpian** cavorters position themselves strategically around the cottage, walloping washtubs, clanking on kettles, and braying like banshees.*

TEMULENT

TEM-yoo-luhnt

adjective

Intoxicated, crapulous, drunk.

From Latin *temulentus* (inebriated), from *temetum* (alcohol, particularly strong wine or mead) + *-ulentus*, variant of *-entus* (suffix of abundance).

"Sooner shall God damn'd Lucifer absolve,
And this eternal orb to air dissolve,
Than I, to frenzy temulent, with love,
False to its palpitating precepts prove."

—W. K. (poetry attributed to THOMAS CHATTERTON),
"To the Editor of the *European Magazine*, Exeter, Feb. 17,
1804," *European Magazine and London Review*, 1804

Temulent as toymakers by midnight, the inebriated noisemakers nevertheless
perform a flawless array of reels, jigs, and marches.

RIDENT

RY-duhnt adjective	**Laughing and cheerful, broadly smiling, and in high spirits.**

From Latin *ridens* (laughing), from *ridere* (to laugh).

"As for Mrs. Mackenzie—the very largest curve that shall not be a caricature, and actually disfigure the widow's countenance—a smile so wide and steady, so exceedingly rident, indeed, as almost to be ridiculous, may be drawn upon her buxom face, if the artist chooses to attempt it as it appeared during the whole of this summer evening, before dinner came (when people ordinarily look very grave), when she was introduced to the company."

—WILLIAM MAKEPEACE THACKERAY, *The Newcomes*, 1854

*Possessed of endless energy, the **rident** revelers clearly have no plans for the morrow, playing music, games, and pranks late into the night.*

SCOLION

SKOH-lee-uhn, *SKOH-lee-ahn* noun	**A song sung at a party or banquet, sometimes improvised, started by one guest and continued in succession by others.**

From Ancient Greek σκόλιον (*skólion*: banquet song), from σκολιός (*skoliós*: crooked, describing the disjointed order of singing).

"The main feature and difficulty of the Scolion, as thus described, was that each singer was bound to follow his predecessor not only in subject but in metre also, and was thus precluded from preparation beforehand."

— GEORGE FARNELL, "BANQUET SONGS—THE SCHOLIA," *Greek Lyric Poetry*, 1891

*Just before dawn, someone starts a **scolion**, and everyone takes a turn until it comes back around to the saucy scoundrel who started it.*

FELICIFIC

FEE-luh-SIH-fik
adjective

Pertaining to or causing happiness.

From Latin *felix* (happy) + *facere* (to make).

"Look widely around and wish well to others; but, mindful how
likely dispersed effort is to be lost, and how ignorant you are of
their feelings and circumstances, concentrate your felicific effort
where you can make tolerably sure that none of it will be lost, and
let your production of happiness be on your own ground, your
contribution to the sum of happiness, your own happiness."

—JOHN GROTE, *A Treatise on the Moral Ideals*, 1865

Sol, the quotidian party-pooper, audaciously threatens to end the
felicific *festivities as he skulks furtively from the east.*

SCOPPERLOIT

SKAH-puhr-loyt

noun, verb

1. **A time of idleness or playtime that might include rowdy, uproarious behavior.**

2. **To engage in rowdy playfulness, to roughhouse.**

From scopperil (a spinning top, a restless creature), from Middle English *scop(e)relle*, from Old Norse *skopa* (to dance, to jump, to play) + Middle English *-il* (suffix of agency) + perhaps loiter (to linger, to stand about idly), from Middle English *loitren*, from Middle Dutch *loteren* (to shake, to wobble).

"Why I ha bin havin a game a skoppoloit along
i th' man Jenkins i' th' chatch yahd."

—JAMES ORCHARD HALLIWELL,
A Dictionary of Archaic & Provincial Words, 1852

Exasperated beyond patience, the beleaguered bookseller wonders, amid the din of the crowd, just how long these rogues intend to **scopperloit** *around the cottage.*

SPREEING COVE

SPREE-ing KOHV

noun

Someone taking delight in a party, a lively reveler.

From Scots *spree* (disturbance, hubbub), from *spreath* (cattle raid), from Old Scots *spreithe* (booty, plunder), from Scots Gaelic *spreidh* (cattle, a cattle dowry), from Middle Irish *preid* (booty), from Latin *praeda* (plunder) + -ing, from Old English -*ing* (verbal suffix) + [pre-1570 thieves' cant] *cove* (man, fellow), from Romani *kova* (that person).

"There was a large batch of 'spreeing coves' brought up before the Recorder yesterday. They occupied the side seat within the bar, and looked like men going through the principal ordeal of sea-sickness."

—DENNIS CORCORAN, "On a Jolly Spree," *Pickings from the Portfolio of the Reporter of the New Orleans "Picayune,"* 1846

A Brobdingnagian **spreeing cove** *declares that the revelers intend to whoop it up until the local constabulary arrives to induce them all to stop.*

GAMESTER

GAYM-stuhr

noun

A merry, frolicsome person.

From game, from Old English *gamen* (amusement, pastime) + -ster, from Middle English *-ester*, from Old English *-estre* (suffix of agency).

"This is the sprightly Lady Hedone; a merry Gamester this; people call her Pleasure."

—THOMAS CAREW, *Coelum Britannicum*, 1640

A Falstaffian **gamester** *laughs heartily and shouts, "You needn't worry, for I am the local constabulary!" before detonating a barrage of fireworks.*

EPINICIAN

eh-pih-NISS-ee-uhn adjective	**Pertaining to or celebrating victory or triumph.**

From Ancient Greek ἐπινίκιος (*epiníkios*: triumphal), from ἐπί (*epi-*: on) + νίκη (*níkē*: victory) + -an, from Old French *-ain*, from Latin *-anus* (adjectival suffix).

"Alkibiadês obtained from Euripidês the honour of an epinikian ode, or song of triumph, to celebrate this event."

— GEORGE GROTE, *A History of Greece*, 1846

Thunderous booms and dazzling lights elicit **epinician** *cheers from anyone still capable of standing.*

NOCEUR

noh-SUHR

noun

A libertine who revels late into the night.

From French *noceur* (nighttime reveler), from Latin *nox* (night) + French *-eur* (suffix of agency), from Old French *-eor*, from Latin *-ator*.

"In Ibsen the characters who bother themselves about the arts are invariably humbugs or hypocrites or *noceurs*, and it would not surprise us to hear that Alving *père* had a nice taste in engravings."

—JAMES AGATE, *Buzz, Buzz! Essays of the Theatre*, 1917

*Around noon, the last reveler—a local **noceur** of rakish repute—regains consciousness, clocks that he's alone, and wambles home to sleep off the woofits.*

OTIOSE

OH-tee-ohs,
OH-shee-uhs

adjective

1. At rest or at ease.

2. Inactive or idle.

3. Unemployed.

From Latin *otiosus* (idle), from *otium* (ease, leisure) + *-osus* (adjectival suffix).

"An otiose God, then, surveying unmoved 'this dusty fuliginous chaos,' is the residuum of all this furious apostrophizing."

—FREDERIC HARRISON, *Froude's Life of Carlyle,* 1886

*With heavy, **otiose** sighs, the newlyweds fall into bed to dream of the future, too tired to hear the ominous skittering coming from beneath the bed.*

GRAMERCIES
(Acknowledgments)

FIRST AND FOREMOST, IMMEASURABLE PRAISE AND gratitude must be heaped lovingly upon my supportive partner in grandiloquence: Angie, my wife. Were it not for her consistent encouragement in times of doubt, Grandiloquent Word of the Day—and by extension, this book—simply wouldn't exist. She selflessly contributed so much of her own time, energy, creativity, editing, proofreading, and help with research over the years to ensure that the enterprise, including calendars, journals, and this book, are the very best that they can be. Thank you, my angel.

A Brobdingnagian thank you to James Jayo and Countryman Press for having the vision to see that Grandiloquent Word of the Day would work as a book. May we enjoy a long and prosperous partnership.

Deep thanks also to our supportive social media community, especially including our wonderful Patreon supporters, as well as those who've contributed to our annual Kickstarters in support of our wall calendars, and of course those who consistently participate in the comments section on Facebook and share our posts to help grow our fan base.

Thank you to my family. I love you.

Thank you to all my friends but especially my Anam Cara. You know who you are.

Thank you to my teachers who cared enough to take the time to get to know me and become a friend: Katie, Rohn, Terry, and Daniel.

CONSEQUENT ERUDITIONS
(Further Reading)

UR SHARED TONGUE STANDS ON THE SHOULDERS of giants. As such, I hereby offer a suggested reading list of books that don't sit on my bookshelf because they live on my desk.

- Linda Berdoll, *Very Nice Ways to Say Very Bad Things*, 2003
- Robert W. Bly, *The Words You Should Know to Sound Smart*, 2009
- Peter Bowler, *The Superior Person's Book of Words*, 1979
- Peter Bowler, *The Superior Person's Second Book of Weird and Wondrous Words*, 1992
- William F. Buckley Jr., *The Lexicon*, 1998
- Josefa H. Byrne, *Mrs. Byrne's Dictionary of Unusual, Obscure, and Preposterous Words*, 1974
- Danny Danziger and Mark McCrum, *The Whatchamacallit*, 2009
- Charles Harrington Elster, *There's a Word for It!: A Grandiloquent Guide to Life*, 1996
- Karen Elizabeth Gordon, *The Disheveled Dictionary*, 1997
- John Koenig, *The Dictionary of Obscure Sorrows*, 2021
- Peter E. Meltzer, *The Thinker's Thesaurus*, 2005
- Peter Novobatzky and Ammon Shea, *Depraved and Insulting English*, 2001
- Russell Rocke, *The Grandiloquent Dictionary*, 1972

- Anything written by Mark Forsyth:

  - *The Etymologicon*, 2011
  - *The Horologicon*, 2012
  - *The Elements of Eloquence*, 2013
  - *The Unknown Unknown*, 2014
  - *A Christmas Cornucopia*, 2016
  - *A Short History of Drunkenness*, 2017
  - his blog, *The Inky Fool*, ongoing

Other resources include:

- English Dialect Society, *Glossaries of Words Used in Mid-Yorkshire and Holderness*, 1876

- James Orchard Halliwell, Esq., F.R.S., *Dictionary of Archaic and Provincial Words, Obsolete Phrases, Proverbs, and Ancient Customs, from the Fourteenth Century*, 1901

- James Halliwell-Phillipps, *A Dictionary of Archaic and Provincial Words, Obsolete Phrases, Proverbs, and Ancient Customs, from the Fourteenth Century*, 1846

- John Camden Hotten, *The Slang Dictionary: Etymological, Historical and Anecdotal*, 1859

- George W. Matsell, *Vocabulum: Or, The Rogue's Lexicon*, 1859

- A. L. Mayhew and Walter W. Skeat, *A Concise Dictionary of Middle English: From A.D. 1150 to 1580*, 1888

- John Walker, *A Critical Pronouncing Dictionary, and Expositor of the English Language*, 1858

- George Watson, *The Roxburghshire Word-book Being a Record of the Special Vernacular Vocabulary of the County of Roxburgh, with an Appendix of Specimens*, 1923

SYSTEMATIZATION
(Index)